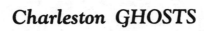

Charleston GHOSTS

CHARLESTON GHOSTS

by MARGARET RHETT MARTIN
illustrated by Alfred Simson

UNIVERSITY OF SOUTH CAROLINA PRESS
Columbia, South Carolina

COPYRIGHT © 1963 by the
UNIVERSITY OF SOUTH CAROLINA PRESS

Published in Columbia, South Carolina

First Printing 1963

Manufactured in the United States of America

99 98   17 16 15

Library of Congress Cataloging Data
Martin, Margaret Rhett.
    Charleston ghosts. Columbia, University of South Carolina Press, 1963
    x, 105 p. illus. 25 cm.
    1. Ghosts. 2. Legends—South Carolina—Charleston. I. Title.
    BF1461.M36   63-22508

ISBN 0–87249–091–2

For My Children

Walter, Helen, Goodwyn, Julius, and Edward Taylor

Contents

PAGE

I. The Ghost at Old House 1

II. The Haunted Avenue 5

III. The Childsbury Tale 11

IV. The Whistling Doctor 17

V. The Man Who Came Back 30

VI. The Thirteenth Step 35

VII. The Wayfarer at Six Mile House 40

VIII. The Passenger from Cuckols Creek 47

IX. The Leaning Tombstone 51

X. The Legend of Fenwick Castle 57

XI. The Ghost of Daughter Dale 63

XII. Mary Hyrne Protests 66

XIII. The Fateful Handkerchief 71

XIV. Medway's Ghosts 83

XV. The Wager of "Mad Archie" Campbell . . . 87

XVI. The Ghost in the Library 92

XVII. The Sword Gates Romance 96

XVIII. Pinky 101

ILLUSTRATIONS

The Haunted Avenue 6

Fenwick Hall 56

Medway 84

I am convinced every old Charleston house has its ghostly visitor. One properly attuned will be aware of its presence.

Introduction

The people in these stories are, or were, *real people*. The houses and plantations they lived in are *real houses* (although some are not still standing). If you can lend me that "willing suspension of disbelief" which Coleridge talks about, you will find in the following pages *real ghosts*.

I believe in ghosts. I *did* see the ghost at *Old House*, which is the subject of the first story. I did not dream it. A dream does not fill one with horror for days, or so unnerve one that no sedative can induce sleep the night after.

Seeing ghosts runs in my family. My mother once saw an old man she'd never laid eyes on before come in and sit in front of the fire at her home at 9 Limehouse Street; then he vanished. It was in the afternoon before the lamps were lit. My brother was awakened once by a sensation of being choked and the sound of a strange humming. He and his friends investigated every logical possibility and found no explanation. He was living then in the Dictator Rutledge house on Broad

Street, and nothing would induce him to risk another such experience there.

I am convinced that every old Charleston house has its ghostly visitor; if one is properly attuned, he will be aware of its presence.

After seeing the ghost at *Old House,* I decided to record my experience and investigate some of the stories of supernatural visitations in which the city and the county of Charleston abound. I have spent much time in research on old histories, wills, and other public records, as well as in interviews.

Most of these stories will indicate in themselves to what extent they are documented. Some of the actions, as I clearly state, are verified in public records—such as the fact that the slave girl in "The Haunted Avenue" stole the jewels of her mistress and set fire to *Belvidere.*

Word-of-mouth documentation was secured for other stories. The strange situation with psychological overtones recounted in "The Fateful Handkerchief" has long been a Charleston mystery. The "real truth" as I tell it was given me by a relative of Francis Simmons, the chief character in the tale. I received documentation for "The Thirteenth Step" from a member of the Jenkins family who had lived at *Brick House* before it was burned and had seen the bloodstain on the stair.

Although it was widely known that Joseph Ladd, "The Whistling Doctor," died following a duel shortly after the Revolution, the full story was harder to round out than any other. I am indebted to *The Literary Remains of Joseph Brown Ladd, M.D.,* a book by his sister, Mrs. Elizabeth Hawkins of Rhode Island, for many facts in my account and for the poems by Joseph Ladd I have quoted. The work (Clinton Hall, N. Y.: H. C. Sleight, 1832) includes a sketch of Ladd's life by W. D. Chittenden.

Other rare books and manuscripts I consulted and the stories they shed light on, include: Fairfax Harrison's *John's Island Stud* (privately printed, Old Dominion Press, 1931) — "The Legend of Fenwick Castle"; Miss Eola Willis' *The*

Charleston Stage in the XVIII Century (The State Co., 1924) —"The Ghost of Daughter Dale" and "The Whistling Doctor"; The Octogenarian Lady's *The Olden Time of Carolina* (Charleston: S. G. Courtenay & Co., 1860)—"Mary Hyrne Protests"; Mrs. Arthur Gordon Rose's *Little Mistress Chicken* (n. pub., n. d.)—"The Childsbury Tale"; Alexander Garden's *Anecdotes of the Revolutionary War in America* (Charleston: A. E. Miller, 1822)—"The Wager of Mad Archie Campbell" and "The Man Who Came Back"; and Mabel Trott Fitz-Simmons' *Hot Words and Hair Triggers* (manuscript on file with the Charleston Library Society, 1938)—"The Whistling Doctor."

Joseph Peeples (Peoples), "The Wayfarer at Six Mile House," was a real person and figured in the trial, and hanging of Lavinia and John Fisher on Feb. 18, 1820, after two skeletons were found near the inn. Purists may say my account does not follow the public records in every respect; they cannot quarrel with my claim, however, that it is the true legend.

But further discussion of *fact* might take us out of that hazy, lamplit, *fanciful* atmosphere conducive to extrasensory perception.

When *Middleton Place* was a ruin, a gentle lady came often to walk the deserted garden paths. Now that the gardens are beautiful, the ghostly visitor is at rest and no longer grieves over the destruction of the flowers she loved. Although I have not included the *Middleton Place* ghost in this book, many of my tales seem to demonstrate the same point: that unhappiness and suffering have attracted other-worldly visitors back to their earthly haunts. However, this cannot be taken as a hard-and-fast rule. A Charleston leader, Colonel Isaac Hayne, comes back to lend strength to those he left behind; a little Dutchman comes back to *Medway* to enjoy a pipe in the fine house he built; a strait-laced old lady comes back to stare when she feels her moral censure is needed; and one ghost comes back strictly for fun.

I wish to acknowledge the encouragement given me by Samuel L. Latimer, Jr. and *The State* newspaper in publishing earlier versions of these stories in the Sunday Magazine Supplement, and also the helpful criticism and instruction of Philip Ketchum and Bob Burtt of The Blue Ridge Writer's Colony in Saluda, North Carolina.

I am indebted to Alfred Simson for his excellent sketches which illustrate this book.

MARGARET RHETT MARTIN.

June 1, 1963.

Charleston GHOSTS

The Ghost at Old House

My week-end visit at *Old House*, which stands in a se-
cluded spot on Edisto Island, was anticipated with
keenest pleasure, for I had never seen the plantation side of
the island. As events transpired, more than the scenery proved
memorable.

It was early September and still oppressively hot, even at
night. I drove for miles over roads bordered by creeks and
marshes and by lush tropical growth until we turned into the
driveway. Suddenly we saw *Old House*, a wooden dwelling
with a piazza across the front surrounded by great moss-hung
oaks that seemed to reach for it with yearning arms.

The unpretentious building, known to be the earliest residence on the island, has only one story and an attic. However,
its fan window, Palladian door, and Doric columns contribute
to its architectural beauty. It stood isolated in the eerie stillness, yet seemed vibrant with some enchantment. It was per-
vaded by a strange aura as of people watching—people, whom

I could neither see nor hear. Even then, at midday with the hot sunshine pouring down, I could feel their presence.

I greeted my hostess and immediately spoke of these haunting fancies. "There must be a ghost?" I asked.

"Oh, yes," she replied carelessly and smiled.

Silence followed.

The gaiety of the party dispelled further imaginings until the late afternoon when everyone else went off for a swim in the creek. I remained behind to rest and enjoy the lovely woods and the deep peace of the countryside. I sat alone on the piazza and gazed with delight upon the tall trees against the sky, the gray-moss drapery, the strong greens of the Cassina bushes, all softened by the failing light and the haze that hovers aboundingly in the Low Country.

In the moody stillness, once more those fancied people crowded around me. Rocking gently, I rested my head against the back of the chair, and, half closing my eyes, I could almost see them. All about they were, on the piazza, coming up the steps, under the oaks. A bird called plaintively from afar. As the afternoon lengthened, the shadows took on more furtive shapes.

What story, I wondered, was associated with this place? I thought of *Brick House*, also on Edisto, where the bride was shot on her wedding night by a childhood friend whose love she spurned. I wished ardently to know what misfortune held the ghost at *Old House*, be it lovely lady in trailing white gown or deserted sweetheart who had died of a broken heart.

The moon came up and dusk gave way to the weird paleness of moonlight. The feeling of expectation increased as the shadows became wilder and more elusive. Surely the ghost would appear. The spell was broken by the return of the party. They joined me on the piazza, and although with much bantering they tried to call forth the apparition, there remained only the shadows, the moonlight, and the stillness.

Bedtime came, and our hostess climbed with me and the friend who would share the room, to the attic above. The small room with dormer windows had an old double bed on one side, and on the other, a single bed against the wall.

Because of the heat our hostess suggested that we leave the door open.

Remembering the dark room across the hall, I answered quickly, "Oh, I think not."

This occasioned a laugh and some joking, and I ended by compromising. I partially closed the door and put a chair against it.

Good nights were said, and our hostess called up to me from downstairs, "You are not in the ghost room!"

My friend was soon asleep, leaving the big bed for me, and I lay awake tossing and turning through the long gray night.

Some time in the dark hours before dawn my unrest grew.

I was lying on my side facing the door, and opening my eyes, I saw a man seated in the chair staring at me. I saw him quite distinctly, a small man in a nondescript gray suit and a gray hat. His eyes were cold and mean and full of hate.

The next moment he was gone.

I then experienced an indescribable sensation, not of fright, nor of horror, but a feeling of violent revulsion. It seemed unbearable, and I threw out my arms and uttered a cry.

My friend did not wake. The night seemed endless in the little room with the darkness and the stillness. If I closed my eyes, or turned away, there was always the impulse to look— and the fear of seeing. But the vision had been so vivid that unless I did look, I would think that the man with the hate-filled eyes was still there. I told myself over and over that it was a dream, knowing full well that I had never gone to sleep. With the dawn, I dozed fitfully until the clock told me that I might venture downstairs. I put on a robe and, after fortifying myself with coffee, joined my hostess on the piazza.

The beautiful daylight was making the world normal again, and I asked, "Is the ghost a man or a woman?"

"A man," she said. "Why?"

"I—I saw him."

She smiled, doubting, and began to quiz me. "What nationality was he?"

I hesitated only a moment, then, remembering the cruel faces of the soldiers of Hitler's army, answered with conviction, "German."

Her eyes grew wide as she gazed at me. When she spoke, her voice was just above a whisper, "It was a German who was murdered in the room across the attic hall."

Then she told the story: Some time after the Confederate War, there had come to this island community a little German. He opened a small grocery store and sold food to the Negroes. Since *Old House* was unoccupied, the owner had been happy to have a tenant and gave the German permission to live in the room upstairs.

The man was a hard dealer. Food was scarce and money scarcer. He took from the Negroes their pennies and gave them as little as possible in return. When they protested, he cursed them and ordered them from his store. Soon, his meanness had worked the poor blacks into a frenzy of hatred.

One night they came, broke into the house, and went up to his room. The German opened his eyes to see huge menacing forms bending over him. He began to curse and, in his usual autocratic way, ordered the intruders to get out.

But this time there was no surly obedience. Instead, the Negroes pulled their knives and stabbed him. They dragged his body down the stairs and threw it into the yard.

Today on the steps, deeply dyeing the wood, are the bloodstains—while from time to time the little man comes back, to haunt and to hate.

The Haunted Avenue

Belvidere, beside the Cooper River three miles from Charleston, had a perfection of plan and detail that bespoke its role in an era of gracious living. From room to room I went one summer's afternoon, many years ago, loath to leave this evidence of a past so full of dignity and beauty.

When I came out, a sunset in its last brilliance illuminated the fine old mansion and darkened, in contrast, the majestic oaks guarding its entrance. The gold soon faded, and the waning light crept in long reaches under the great arms of the trees to touch the mellow walls and to purple the marshes spreading to the river.

I stood until the soft dusk covered everything, and there was only a tilted moon in a pale sky. I was bemused by the *Belvidere* legend: under the oaks at night a chuck-will's-widow calls from the distance and a ghostly strangeness closes in. Something comes stealthily along the avenue. A sensation of tingling cold creeps up the visitor's spine, leaving him

THE HAUNTED AVENUE

"*. . . so close that I could have reached out and touched it.*"

powerless to move. The *thing* sways so close that one can almost reach out and touch it—whatever it is. There is no definite shape to be seen, only a dark form and white eyeballs and staring eyes.

Even as one looks, it passes and vanishes. It is the ghost of a slave girl forever reliving her strange shadow play.

It began on a bright day in March, 1796, when Timothy Wale strode vigorously along the avenue, a hoe on his shoulder and purpose in his stride; but there was no song in his heart for he was only the gardener for a wealthy planter. It was a pleasant life, but he was not content to be a workman on another man's estate. This beauty, this wealth, this important property with which he was associated, were possessed by Colonel Thomas Shubrick. And Wale, who had come to the new country to make his fortune, was only a garden man with no immediate prospects of betterment.

Memories of his life in England still filled him with bitterness. He remembered well the long years of struggle when his pale, sickly mother gave all of her strength to provide for her children, earning a pittance that would scarcely buy bread and gruel for five hungry mouths. His brothers had wasted away with tuberculosis. His beautiful sweetheart Clarissa of the raven hair and blue eyes had also been a victim of the disease. After the loss of Clarissa, he had decided to take up life in a faraway country. In America he had hoped to get ahead, to find peace, a good living, and a measure of happiness. Instead, he had found hard work on a rich man's estate—and loneliness, for there were no friendly associates on the estate for the immigrant gardener.

On around the circling avenue he walked, intent on reaching the walled garden beside the mansion.

"Belvidere," he said to himself, and he liked the sound of it.

It was a beautiful and desirable property with vast stretches of grass on three sides, the blue sky hanging over fields and distant marshes, and the handsome house, itself, with its spacious rooms.

Timothy came to the place beneath an oak where a **Negro** girl stood. One of the slaves serving "the Missus," she was tall and well-formed. Her breasts showed high and round under her calico dress as she flattened herself against the broad trunk of the tree. Timothy Wale had already noticed this girl, who, strangely enough, was also named Clarissa— and, as before, she stared impudently at him, her lips spreading in a slow smile.

He looked away, refusing to see her, and hurried on. Reaching the garden, he seized his hoe and struck out at the weeds between his rows of bulbs. The narcissuses were in full bloom and, with the purple violets, painted the enclosure in bright patches.

Soon the girl was there, coming in timidly and stooping to pick blossoms with quick, sure fingers. She, too, was in need of a friend, for she could see ahead only the bleak existence of a slave, and this strange man, this Englishman—handsome, too, in his tall, lanky way—offered a vague hope of something better. If only she could awaken his interest, if only she could make him see their need, each for the other! Once more she paused and stared at him, and when he raised his eyes, she dropped hers with a knowing smile and reached for another violet.

He stole furtive glances at her, wondering. Presently he walked past and, speaking without turning or looking at her, said, "Tonight. At the end of the avenue."

She smiled and gave no sign of hearing.

That night, the man waited beneath the trees, listening. He heard only the chirping of crickets and the singing of the frogs. Would she come?

A fitful breeze stirred the leaves. He stared at the night and could see nothing. Rubbing his hands on his hips in disgust, he thought of leaving; then, in the darkness, there was a swift movement, and she was there against him. He reached for her, feeling her warm softness and her hot breath upon his cheek.

"Take me away from here," she pleaded. "Take Clarissa away."

At his remonstrances, she clutched at him, begging him not to leave her. But Timothy laughed and repeated his protest that he had no means.

"Clarissa get means. Missus got jew'ls, en de box. Clarissa get 'em fer ye. Den ye take me wid ye?"

Timothy's hands tightened on her arms. Here was his chance. Jewels!

"Can you get them?" he asked, and when she assented, he urged, "Get them, Clarissa! Get them for me. Listen—wrap them in your kerchief, and bring them to me here. We will go where no one will find us. We will be rich, Girl. Hear me? Rich."

"I get 'em, sure—de fust day de Missus go ter town."

On Saturday, Mrs. Shubrick ordered the coach and set out for Charleston to do some shopping. The slave girl watched and soon found the chance to be alone in the big bedroom. She took the key from the drawer where it lay hidden and unlocked the chest. Her eyes grew big at what she saw—brooches and rings and necklaces and even a tiara.

Her fingers were trembling as she spread out her kerchief on the floor and filled it with the beautiful gems in their costly settings. The chest was quickly locked again and the key replaced. She tied the jewels into a bundle and took them to her cabin in the slave quarters.

All was dark and quiet when Clarissa slipped out to see the gardener, clutching the precious loot to her as she ran.

Timothy came to meet her and, stretching out his hand in the darkness, found the bundle and seized it, saying with great gladness, "Ah, you clever girl!"

"Now, we go," she whispered, clinging to him.

"No—" he pushed her back. "I cannot take you." And when she held on to him, he said sharply, "Don't you know that they would come after you? Don't you know that we would be caught and brought back, and you would be whipped? Now, listen. I will send for you later."

Clarissa clutched wildly at his coat, but he was too quick for her. He loosened her hands and fled, disappearing into the night. Throwing herself upon the ground, she beat the turf with her hands and uttered smothered groans. He was gone—gone—and she would have to stay.

In panic, she got to her feet and stumbled to her cabin, where all night she lay on the cot shaking and groaning. By morning she had a plan.

She kept to her bed and wailed, pretending she had a "misery"; they sent Aunt Sibbie to dose her. Later, when Clarissa heard the coach come and take the Shubricks off to church, she stole out, knowing that at this time the slaves would be busy in the kitchen. She ran quickly up the stairs and into her mistress' bedroom.

"Ef de house done bu'nt, nobody know dat de jew'ls is gone," she thought.

Moving with desperate haste, she got papers, letters—anything that would burn—and, piling them against the wall, set them afire.

For a brief time she stood and watched, until she saw the flames gain headway and start licking at the curtains and the woodwork. She fled, to hide once more in the cabin, burying her head beneath a quilt.

Returning from service, the Shubricks saw the smoke from afar and in fearful apprehension urged the horses on. Upon turning into the avenue, they caught sight of the smoldering ruins of their beautiful home.

Suspicion pointed to the strange behavior of the slave girl. When she was arrested and tried, she broke down and confessed to both crimes and was hanged.

The lonely cry of the chuck-will's-widow trembles on the night where even the rebuilt *Belvidere* no longer remains. The visitor hastens away—away from the haunted avenue—from Clarissa's ghost waiting for the English gardener who never came back.

The Childsbury Tale

It was a day in early spring in 1752 when the cold had suddenly been replaced with a warm, magnetic sunshine that drew the young-at-heart outdoors. In the village of Childsbury, Madame Dutarque returned from her marketing to find the house strangely quiet, and apparently empty as well. Mr. Mack, the roomer, would be away at this hour, but the child should be there. She had been instructed to stay in and sew a long seam. It was punishment, and well-deserved, for her persistent idleness.

Madame Dutarque went from room to room, hurriedly searching, until she came to a closed door. Here she paused and put her ear against it to listen. In there her husband would be poring over his beloved Plato. She knew that any interruption annoyed him and would be the occasion for an ugly scene. She knew, moreover, that his temper when aroused was to be feared; he heaped up hurtful words on his opponents and sometimes followed them with crueler deeds. However, her fear for the child's welfare was greater than dread of her husband's anger, and she summoned up courage to tap on the door.

Opening it timidly, she asked in her whining voice, "Where is the child?"

The man sitting at the desk wheeled around impatiently, stared at her blankly and roared, "How should I know?"

"But—I left her here. I told her to stay indoors and sew a long seam."

They looked at each other in exasperation. Was it not enough to teach the brats in the Childsbury school? To have to take this one to live in was too much. It was more than they could bear—only, it paid well—it paid very well.

"No doubt she will return soon," and with this comment, Monsieur Dutarque dismissed the subject to resume his reading.

Dinnertime came. When they had eaten and there was still no sign of Catherine, the wife insisted that her schoolmaster-husband go in search of the child. With much ill-humor, he took his horse pistols and a rope and set out.

The child was only eight years old and could not have gone far. It was some time, however, before he found her, in a grove of oaks in the town square. In her long muslin dress, now mussed and dirty, she was seated at the foot of a great tree playing with a tiny cooter.

He had nearly reached her when she looked up. She sprang to her feet in alarm at the sight of his face which was livid with rage. He wanted to lash out at the annoying child, to beat her. Only the thought of her family deterred him, for her grandfather had owned the whole village of Childsbury and her mother, who lived now at the beautiful *Kensington Plantation*, dispensed coin generously for the child's upkeep.

"What do you mean, running away like this?" he snarled.

The child gazed at him with resentment, "I wanted to be outdoors."

"Outdoors," mimicked the angry man. "Outdoors, is it? Ye shall have outdoors."

He took her by the arm and dragged her through the quiet street, just beyond the village, to the burying ground where he bound her with the rope to a tombstone.

"That will teach her a lesson—to leave her there for awhile," he thought. Before dark he would return and get her.

He tied the rope tightly, pinning her hands behind her back, her shoulders firmly against the stone.

"Now," he sneered. "When ye have had enough, ye call. Maybe I come—eh?"

Then he stamped away, deaf to the childish voice calling after, "M'sieu Dutarque—M'sieu Dutarque—Dear M'sieu Dutarque." It followed him all the way down the street as he strode away, "M'sieu Dutar—que—."

He hurried back to his reading, calling to his wife, "She is safe," and closed the door upon further inquiry.

Madame Dutarque went about her work satisfied.

Catherine struggled to be free, but she could scarcely move, so tightly was she bound.

She thought of her mother and her heart cried out. "Why did she let this happen to me? Why—why—why—? Why did my dear father have to die fighting Indians? Why did Mr. Ball have to come when I was so happy with my mother? Why did my mother have to marry him?

"And why—why did she have to get a new baby, and send me to live with M'sieu and Madame Dutarque? They do not love me. They are cross—and now they have tied me up to get rid of me!"

Tears streamed down her cheeks. They tasted salty on her lips. Her little body shook with sobs. Presently she went to sleep.

When she awoke, it was quite dark. The rope cutting her arms brought immediate awareness of where she was. The darkness terrified her. Turning her eyes from side to side, she thought of stories she had heard from the Negroes, of bears and Indians, and of ghosts. She could hear the bark of a fox and the distant baying of a wolf; and the scary hooting of a screech owl. Her flesh tingled with horror.

Out of the night came the voice of a Negro, "Lord, hab mussy," and the voice sounded afraid.

Then she saw the devil head. She knew it came from hell because its eyes were still on fire. And the huge head glowed like hot coals. It was coming straight at her!

"M'sieu Dutarque!" she shrieked. "Come get me! Dear M'sieu Dutarque!"

The goblin hesitated, seeming to stare at her—then came on faster. She thought of Mr. Mack who had a room at the Dutarques'. Kind Mr. Mack.

"Oh, Mr. Mack! Mr. Mack!" she screamed.

And the terrible head came nearer.

"I will be good—."

Its staring eyes and grinning mouth were almost upon her. She uttered one last piteous wail, "Ma—ma—," and fell unconscious with her head against the rope.

But kind Mr. Mack had waked in the still night and heard her cry. He recognized her voice, and, leaping from his bed, ran to her empty room. He went then to rouse the schoolmaster, but the wife awoke instead and tried to deter him. He could not have heard Catherine's cries, she said, for the child was with her aunt at *Fish Pond Plantation*.

Mr. Mack could not forget that appealing little voice crying in the night. He hurried into his clothes and ran out through the street calling, "Catherine! Catherine!!"

Not finding her, he saddled a horse and rode to *Fish Pond*. There, Catherine's aunt and uncle were truly alarmed, and roused half the countryside. Before dawn a sizable group were on the move. With lanterns and hounds, they set out to find the child.

When Moony, the slave, saw them coming into Childsbury, he was afraid and hid. He had been out that night without a permit and, to assure his getting by unquestioned, had made a false face out of a giant gourd, cutting slits for eyes and mouth; in it he had fastened a lighted candle. Passing the cemetery, Moony heard the child cry, and his impulse was to go to her. He forgot the terrifying object he was carrying.

Upon reaching her, he found her so still and cold he thought she must be dead. Then, in mortal terror, fearing that somehow he would be blamed, he hid in the bushes and watched. At sight of the search party, in the light of early morning when his permit was not in question, he decided to be helpful. Rushing out, he clutched at the bridle of the first horse and cried, "Leetle Mis' Cat'rin en de grabeya'd, dead an' cold."

They found her, untied the rope and took her limp body to the schoolmaster's house. But Monsieur and Madame Dutarque were nowhere to be seen. Awakened by the baying of the hounds, the two had dressed and fled in panic.

Catherine was put to bed. They rubbed her inert arms and forced wine between her lips, but they could not rouse her; they got a coach and took her to *Kensington* to her mother.

When they turned into the long avenue, her mother came running to meet her and, catching her daughter to her heart, hugged her and cried her name.

Catherine opened her eyes and her lips formed, in her sweet childish voice, the words, "Dear M'sieu Dutarque."

That was all. Not until the following day did she speak again. Then, surrounded by love and kindness, she smiled at them.

Suddenly, with great effort, she said in a strange voice, "Don't let them hurt poor M'sieu Dutarque."

Those words saved the schoolmaster's life. He had finally been captured near the river trying to get across, and was brought back to face the angry men.

Before them he stood trembling, knowing in his wretchedness that the whipping he would get would probably be the death of him. Then into their midst rode a gentleman waving a letter and crying, "Hold!"

It was Mr. Ball, who had ridden hard to overtake them.

"It is written here," he said. "Catherine has her voice, and she prays that you do not harm Monsieur Dutarque."

There was a great murmur of protest, but in the end they agreed to abide by her wishes. They took the schoolmaster, stripped him of his wig and his long-skirted coat, and tied him tailwise on a mule. The animal stretched out its hind legs and the crowd shouted derision. The drummer boys beat a "rub-a-dub-a-dub," and the frightened animal raced madly for the river. The men hooted and booed. No one knew or cared what became of Monsieur or Madame Dutarque.

Catherine Chicken grew up and married Benjamin Simons of *Middleburg Plantation* on Cooper River. Her portrait, hanging there still, shows grave eyes and a wistful droop to the sweet lips, for Catherine never forgot her night of terror in the Childsbury graveyard.

A *duel at dawn behind the old*
barracks solved his problems

IV

The Whistling Doctor

Twilight fell upon church street like a soft cloak, enveloping in shadow its vine-covered walls and narrow sidewalks and muffling its timeworn cobblestones. I searched in the deepening dusk for Number 59, which I expected to be gray and gloomy and, probably, somewhat dilapidated.

To my surprise, I found the house with its fresh coat of new ochre paint and a gleaming white door was beautiful even in the waning light. The white door, faced with columns, opened on a wide piazza from which one entered a garden filled with dark trees. Brooding memories could very well haunt such a spot; however, I turned back to the house.

I discovered the true front door in the center of the structure, a location which is typical of Charleston houses. Upon being admitted, I saw in the mellow lamplight a hallway with spacious rooms on either side. At the end of the hall was a staircase with paneled stairwell and rail and banisters of black walnut. There was no carpet on the polished floor or stairs.

The house seemed a proper environment for normalcy and contentment. But the hall and stairs are said to echo yet with a plaintive tune whistled long ago and the whistler's ill-fated foot steps on fortune's treadmill.

On a certain bright day, in the year 1783, a young man stepped eagerly out of a stagecoach at Charleston. Though his green cloth coat and his white shirt frills were rumpled, he would attract attention anywhere, first for his youth—scarce twenty years had he seen—and for his good looks. His manner, too, was noticeable, for he was gentle and courteous. He stretched himself and stamped his feet, glad to end the long journey, for he had come all the way from Newport, Rhode Island.

Day by day his heart had grown heavier as he saw the miles go by, for every turn of the wheels took him further away from the girl he loved. Day by day as the rumbling coach jolted over the rough roads, he had sat swaying, remembering her soft blond hair and the gentle sweetness of her blue eyes.

He recalled their first meeting, a year before, in the Redwood Library when he had stood near as she asked for Spenser's *Faerie Queene*. He, God knows where he had found the courage, had dared to quote from it,

"All that in this delightfull Gardin growes,
    Should happier be, and have immortall bliss."

And when she, in surprise, had turned to him, he had asked, "You are fond of poetry?"

"Yes, I am," she had answered. "It is a beautiful form of expression. And you?"

"I—I make poor attempts to write it," he had admitted.

And she had said, "Oh?—I would like to read your poems."

"You are indeed kind."

"Do you live here?"

"I am Joseph Ladd, and I am studying medicine with Dr. Senter."

"Dr. Senter? He was my father's dearest friend." And smiling graciously, she had added, "Mr. Ladd, I should be happy to have you call and bring your poems. Tomorrow, shall we say—at four?"

There had followed many calls and many more poems, now written to Amanda, for, from the first moment he saw her, she had completely filled his mind.

He had cursed the circumstances that made her an orphan and placed her in the care of an unscrupulous guardian. That grasping person, enjoying with his family many comforts from the management of her fortune, had refused all offers for her hand. When, in defiance, she had declared her love for Joseph, the guardian and his unpleasant relatives had maliciously spread unkind and untrue tales about him. His Amanda, bless her, had not believed a word of them, and they had become secretly engaged.

But when would they ever be able to marry? He still had to become established in his profession. Nor could he forget the bitter struggle he had already had. He remembered his despair when he was fourteen and his father had seen fit to buy the farm. Poor Papa, he had not made a success of anything that he had undertaken. They had always been poor, and with no means, it had been impossible for Joseph to obtain the education he so earnestly desired. His only hope was to acquire learning by his own reading and studying. How he had hated the work on the farm that interfered with his progress!

Gazing out of the coach window, he had caught sight of a grove of alders and smiled, remembering with a tinge of pleasure how he had fitted up a study in a clump of alder bushes on the farm. To his great satisfaction, it had never been discovered. There, in his secret haven, he had spent many wonderful hours with his favorite authors.

When his father had finally rebuked him for neglecting his farm duties, he had replied, "My head, Sir, not my hands, must support me." After that, his angry parent had put him in the office of Dr. Senter to study medicine. He was fifteen then, and now, here he was—a full-fledged doctor setting out to make his fortune.

The long journey, the jolting, the weariness, and the monotony were all behind him; he looked with interest at his surroundings. The coach stop was at a small tavern with tabby walls on the outskirts of the city.

He hesitated, and finding himself standing beside the driver who had climbed down from his high seat to watch the passengers alight, turned to him saying, "I suppose I can get a room here for the night?"

The man licked his thin lips and blinked his shifty eyes. Slowly a smile spread over his sunburnt features. "No, Sir, this ain't a fittin' place for a gentleman," he said. Jones' Tavern es what ye want. Jes' tell a coachman to take ye ter Jones' on Meeting Street. Thomas Jones is the man."

In the doorway of the tavern a man stood idly watching the arrival of the coach. He was of medium height, stockily built, and his black hair gleamed in the sunlight. His nose was long and high-bridged, and while his mouth betrayed a certain pettishness, his gray eyes were intelligent and keen. Overhearing the exchange between the handsome stranger and the coachman, he crossed the courtyard with long strides.

Bowing to the newcomer, he said pleasantly, "Perhaps I can be of service to you. My name is Isaacs—Ralph Isaacs."

"Thank you, Mr. Isaacs. I need a place to stay the night, until I can find permanent lodgings. This fellow has kindly directed me to an address."

"Young man," said Isaacs, "I see that you are a stranger here. That place would not be suitable. If you were lucky enough to come away with your life, you most certainly, in any event would have lost all of your possessions. I've a mind to have the fellow horsewhipped!"

The driver, in terror, backed away and broke into a run, disappearing behind the building.

The young doctor, astonished, watched him go, then laughing, turned to Isaacs and said, "I see that I am deeply indebted to you, Sir. My name is Joseph Brown Ladd. I am a doctor, and have come from Rhode Island to settle in your city. You see, my father's friend, General Nathaniel Greene—he fought the war in this section, you know—thought that I would like it here in Carolina. I have a letter from him, but now I must wash up and get a bite to eat."

"Dr. Ladd, Sir, we are glad to have you in our city, but I must warn you about conditions here," said Isaacs. "It is not safe to go alone on the streets at night, or in certain sections such as Jones's place, or upper Meeting Street, even in the daytime."

Joseph thanked him and said good day, but Isaacs insisted upon accompanying him. Having secured a coach, in which was placed Ladd's traveling bag, he directed the driver to go to the Old Corner Tavern at Broad and Church streets.

During the leisurely drive through the city, Joseph looked about with interest as Isaacs pointed out the streets and buildings. So this was Charleston, this city only just recovering from the devastating effects of the war! The place was still in ruins. Hardly a house above Broad Street had not been damaged by enemy guns, and Isaacs told him he would not find conditions much better in the lower section.

Isaacs' witty conversation about the historic town and its people proved entertaining. Joseph, no longer friendless and alone, warmed to a feeling of agreeable comradeship. He was also profoundly grateful for the intervention that had saved him from thieves and cutthroats at Jones's Tavern. As for Isaacs, the man was flattered and frankly delighted at the friendly attitude of the admirable stranger.

Next day, Joseph set out to deliver his letter to the old ladies, Miss Fannie and Miss Dellie Rose, friends of General Greene. They lived in a beautiful house built by their grandfather, Thomas Rose, and situated below the tavern, in the old section of Church Street. He found the ladies hospitable and charming, and before the visit was over, it was arranged that he would take a room in their home. Money was hard to come by at this period, and the new boarder was a godsend to the impoverished old ladies.

Joseph thought himself lucky when he moved in next day and, for the first time, mounted the steps at the back of the hall. Both old ladies accompanied him to his room, fussing over him, and hoping he would be comfortable. From that moment they adopted him. He became the absorbing delight of their romantic old hearts. They looked forward to his homecoming at night, and when they heard him bounding up the stairs whistling a quaint old English ballad, the austere ladies would shake their heads and smile, noticing it was always the same tune.

The letter of General Greene assured Dr. Ladd of patronage. With his engaging manner and success in treating difficult cases, he soon built a reputation; his practice grew with astonishing rapidity. He took part, not only in the social life of the city, but in its political life and was frequently called upon to make speeches.

Nothing interfered with his writing to Amanda. After whistling his way up the stairs, he spent hours at night in his room pouring out his heart in protestations of love. From "Arouet to Amanda," he wrote,

> Ah, think not absence can afford a cure
> To the sharp woes—the sorrows I endure.
> Amanda, No: 'Twill but augment distress
> To such a height, no mortal can express.
> My soul, distracted, still is fixed on you,
> Was ever heart so wretched and so true?

He sent her poems to fill a volume, begging her to remember him, so far away—"The wretched youth on Carolina's plains." And always he deplored the distance that separated them, "Whence Arouet never, never may return."

Another time he told her that it was not for her beauty alone that he loved her:

Fair as thou art, possessed of every charm—
Of pleasing form and of bewitching face,
Possessed of these alone, you could not move
My faithful heart to such excessive love.

Those charms which beautify the nobler part
Which shine, fair maid: which centre at your heart,
These are the charms which captivate my mind,
These are the charms which my affection bind.[1]

Isaacs did not understand why his friend must spend so many nights at home. He sought Joseph's company incessantly, and their friendship became close. But with the many activities in which the young doctor soon became involved, there was not time for the companionship Isaacs desired. He became jealous of the younger man's popularity, and, since his own lower station prevented his taking full part in the social life of the city, he became resentful and petulant.

While Joseph kept most of his evenings for the composing of love poems, there was not, as a matter of fact, much entertainment for Isaacs to suggest. The concerts twice a week which Joseph occasionally attended, were confined to the social set. The handsome theatre on Dock Street had been burned in the disastrous fire of 1782. There had been nothing to replace it until a Mr. Partridge announced that he would, "by permission," present: a famous singer, a display of horsemanship, and himself dancing a hornpipe on twelve eggs—which he "did to admiration," according to a newspaper account.

This performance took place in the old Exchange Building at the end of Broad Street which had been done over for the occasion. Joseph attended with Isaacs, and, for that evening, the latter was in a happy frame of mind. His countenance shone with benevolence and good humor.

At this time theatres were discouraged. Philadelphia and some other cities had legislated against the showing of plays.

---

[1] Mrs. Elizabeth Hawkins, *The Literary Remains of Joseph Brown Ladd, M.D.* (Clinton Hall, N. Y.: H. C. Sleight, 1832).

However, a Mr. Godwin, an actor of considerable experience, encouraged by the success of Mr. Partridge, came from Savannah, and determined to open a place of entertainment. He chose for the site of his building, Louisburg, outside the city limits at the corner of Meeting and Calhoun streets. In this way he escaped the tax of one hundred pounds sterling, and, since he would give "Entertainments for Representation and Harmony," he called it "Harmony House."

The opening took place on July 11, 1786, and once more, Isaacs and Joseph were seen together. There was a grand concert, a hornpipe, and a pantomime dance. This entertainment was so enthusiastically received that Mr. Godwin's theatre was assured of a successful season. Soon, he began to introduce short plays. These proved so popular that he had trouble getting actors to play the parts and had to resort to amateurs. Local dramatic aspirants included a Miss Barrett, lately arrived in the city, whose first appearance was noted favorably by the *Gazette of the State of South Carolina,* the local paper: "Her figure is good and she promises to become an entertaining and useful actress."

The following month, Mr. Godwin announced a benefit for himself and chose for the play, *Richard III.* Miss Barrett in the role of Anne, the Queen, was to complement his own portrayal of Richard.

Charleston was filled with anticipation over seeing Shakespeare, and for this night, the boxes were all taken and the pit filled to capacity. Joseph had been invited to sit in a box with a party of friends, and Isaacs had to occupy a seat below them. The latter's ill-humor was evident; he kept his eyes away from the gay company that filled the boxes. The ladies fluttered their fans constantly in the oppressive heat. The candles, burning steadily, only added to the discomfort in the crowded theatre. Joseph, wearing with distinction his broad-lapelled coat and ruffled shirt with its high collar, remarked to the lady beside him, "At least, Ma'am, we are spared the torture of wearing powdered wigs."

The play began, and Mr. Godwin gave a splendid perform-ance. As Shakespeare's crafty tyrant, he won bursts of ap-plause, but the poor little amateur Miss Barrett was hope-lessly inadequate. She spoke so low that she could be heard with difficulty even by those in the first rows.

Throughout the evening, Isaacs' displeasure mounted. While seeming not to look at his friend, he was conscious of his every move. It irked him that he, himself, was not considered good enough to associate with these society blades. He was not well-born. Just an average man he was—not good enough for Charleston high society.

Joseph, meeting Isaacs during an intermission, was shocked at the rude rebuff his friendly greeting drew. He was sur-prised at Isaacs' oblique references to "fine friends" and "no time for the likes of me." The curtain was going up, however, and, until the end of the play, Joseph could do nothing to help his friend's state of mind.

After the performance, Joseph, waiting in the lobby for Isaacs, suggested that they walk home together. The latter ungraciously agreed, and Joseph led the way into the open. It was a great relief to feel the fresh breeze from the water, but nothing could cool Isaacs' wrath or calm his resentment. As they walked through the dark streets, picking their way around mud holes and refuse, Joseph repeatedly tried to make conversation, but the older man's pique permitted him only grunts or complaining comments in response. Nothing seemed to interest Isaacs until Joseph spoke of Godwin's "inspired acting."

"Yes," shouted Isaacs, "it was. What a pity the play was spoiled by the stupid performance of that woman. Zounds, anyone could have done better! That languid manner," he mimicked her closing lines, "and the same gestures for every speech. She—"

"You are too hard on the poor girl. Shakespeare did not make it much of a part. She did well considering her lack of experience."

"How can you say that? She was undeniably poor. She spoke too low. She missed her lines. She was wooden in the scene with Richard." He added bitterly, "Maybe fine people are like that and I wouldn't know."

"I didn't notice."

"I'm sure you didn't."

"I liked her. She has a good figure."

"What's that got to do with it? You have some interest in the lady, eh?"

Joseph protested patiently, "Don't be a fool, Isaacs. I do not know her, nor do I wish to make her acquaintance. You know that."

"Oh, I'm a fool, no doubt. But that little ninny is no actress."

Here they reached the corner where their paths diverged.

Joseph paused, and in the darkness, his kindly voice admonished gently, "Well, my friend, I have a right to my opinion. I thought the girl did pretty well. It does seem a pity to ruin her career. Give her a chance, I say."

"I am aware that only the well-born have a right to an opinion. But, nevertheless, I cannot help being able to distinguish between good and bad acting. I say that the little creature should not be allowed to appear again."

"Ah—but don't be so unkind! Have you no mercy? I wouldn't have thought it of you, Isaacs. Sleep over it, Man. Good night."

"Good night, and mercy be damned! I shall not change my lowborn opinion."

Joseph was genuinely distressed by his friend's caustic words. He found it hard to believe that such bitter feeling was harbored in the man's breast. Isaacs had been a devoted friend, and Joseph deplored this new resentment—this animosity that appeared to obsess him. He felt certain that in the light of morning, it would all seem trivial and childish.

Not so with Ralph Isaacs. The wrath increased in his mind and heart. He took to avoiding Joseph and spoke of him in scathing terms to anyone who would listen. At first his anger showed in slighting remarks, but soon there came serious innuendos. Before long Isaacs' accusations became so virulent that Joseph's friends could no longer keep them from him. His only recourse seemed to be publication of a statement in the paper. To the *Gazette* of Charleston, therefore, he wrote a protest against Isaacs' conduct in which he declared, "I account it one of the misfortunes of my life that I became intimate with such a man."

Ralph Isaacs, worked up to a new pitch of fury and hate, came back with a published reply: "I dare affirm that the event of a little time will convince the world that the self-created doctor is as blasted a scoundrel as ever disgraced humanity."

It was now a matter of honor, and Joseph's friends advised that he must send a challenge. Joseph protested that he did not want to fight, and that, in any circumstances, he would not kill. But his friends convinced him that in no other way could he defend his honor. Seconds were secured and the duel arranged for dawn behind the old barracks.

That last night, sleep eluded Joseph, and he turned to poetry for solace. In the long wakeful hours he sensed that events in the offing might still his pen and his longing for Amanda:

> Death, friendly death may soon relieve my pain,
> Long, sure, he cannot be implored in vain.
> Soon, the grim angel will restore my peace,
> Soothe my hard fate, and bid my sorrows cease;
> And tear Amanda's image from my breast.

And then in anguish, he wrote finally:

> When deep oblivion wraps my mind in night,
> When death's dark shadows swim before my sight,
> Will, then, Amanda? Ah, she will I trust,
> Pay the last tribute to my clay-cold dust.
> Will, sighing, say, There his last scene is o'er,
> Who loved as mortal never loved before.

O'er my lone tomb oh, yield that sad relief,
Breathe that soft sigh and pour out all your grief,
Or, shed one tear in pity as you pass,
And just remember that your Arouet was.[2]

Time moved on relentlessly. As the hour approached and the first traces of dawn lightened the sky, a peace lay over the earth. Land and marsh were in deep shadow; the river was a pale ribbon in a sea of mist. A bird passed in swift flight, flashing momentarily as it caught the light.

Two shadows behind the old barracks took on clearer, human outlines. More forms emerged—to stand apart, to meet in whispered conference—before daylight revealed faces grim and gray with concern. One face wore an air of braggadocio and a fixed smile of scorn and bitterness.

About it all was a strangeness—an unreality. Joseph wondered why this was happening to him. He did not hate this man who would oppose him on the field. He was his friend. He kept wanting to accost his antagonist and say, "Isaacs, this is preposterous—our shooting at each other. I am Joseph and you are the man who first befriended me in this city. For this kindness I shall always be grateful."

The seconds came to alert the duelers, and Joseph made an offer to fire hand-to-hand. His bravery was recognized, but his proposal was refused. Joseph was left standing, numbly waiting, while the seconds examined the pistols. When the two main participants received their weapons, they went over to open, level ground and stood, back to back.

Time seemed to pause. There was absolute stillness: even the elements seemed hushed by the enormity of the impending event.

However regrettable the seconds found the affair, they nevertheless gave the signal to march.

The two one-time friends sprang into motion. They paced the twenty steps agreed upon, turned, and faced each other.

---

[2] Mrs. Elizabeth Hawkins, *The Literary Remains of Joseph Brown Ladd, M.D.* (Clinton Hall, N. Y.: H. C. Sleight, 1832).

Joseph raised his gun and fired into the air. If die he must, he could not bring himself to kill. Lowering his arm, he remained motionless, head high, eyes fixed steadily upon his opponent, and waited.

His mind was set in poignant regret upon Amanda—never to see her again—never, never to hold her in his arms. So great was his longing that he wished passionately for the end. Why did Isaacs take so long?

His opponent slowly raised his arm and, with consuming hatred in his eyes, took aim. Two shots rang out in quick succession as the small group of onlookers gasped in horror. Joseph fell under the shock of impact and pain as he went into oblivion. He had been shot in both legs below the knees. It had been Isaacs' intent to cripple him for life.

His friends stopped the bleeding as best they could and took him to his room in the house on Church Street. Miss Fannie and Miss Dellie nursed him, hovering over him, distraught, seeing him grow weaker each day, hearing him call in his delirium for "Amanda—dear Amanda," and listening to his protestations of undying love for her.

They wrote urging Amanda to come, but no tears, frantic pleas nor threats could move her guardian; he had her watched by day and locked in her room by night.

All of Charleston waited in sorrowful concern as the weeks passed and Joseph's life slowly ebbed away. Then he was gone, leaving for Amanda his cry from the heart, "Shed one tear in pity as you pass."

Joseph's lonely spirit never finds peace, for in the house in Church Street his footfalls still echo on the stairs. Footsteps, a rush of tomblike cold air, and a softly whistled tune perpetuate his plaint: "Remember . . . Arouet was."

V

The Man Who Came Back

The Revolutionary hero, Colonel Isaac Hayne, promised to return if he could—and return he did for nearly a hundred years to a house at the corner of Meeting and Atlantic streets.

It was a house he passed on the way to meet his destiny—a fate the enemy decreed for him to help break the rebels' spirit.

When the British took Charles Town in 1780, they permitted the garrisoned American soldiers to return to their homes as prisoners on parole. This parole "shall secure them from being molested in their property by the British troops," Article IV of the Capitulation stated.

The British violated this agreement from the start. Governor John Rutledge told the General Assembly a few years later: "Many of our worthiest citizens, without cause, were long and closely confined—some on board prison ships, and others in the town and castle of St. Augustine; their property disposed of at the will and caprice of the enemy and their families sent to a different and distant part of the continent, without means of support. Many who had surrendered prisoners of war were killed in cold blood. Several suffered death in the most ignominious manner, and others were delivered up to savages and put to tortures under which they expired."

This and much more, the British did, behaving with the "insolent pride of conquerors." And, seeing that the British had broken the good faith over and over again in a brutal manner, many of the patriots felt they were no longer bound by the agreement and were justified in taking up arms again, —such men as Hampton and Pickens and Colonel Isaac Hayne.

Colonel Hayne had retired to his plantation in St. Paul's Parish, where his family had been stricken with smallpox. One child had died, two were very ill, and his wife's life hung in the balance. In the midst of his anxiety and despair, Colonel Hayne received a summons that tore him from his wife's bedside. He was forced to go to Charleston to report to the British and to answer the query, "Will you or will you not become the subject of his Majesty?"

With a heavy heart, Colonel Hayne left his home and set out for the city. There he was told that he must sign a paper declaring himself a British subject, but that he could rest assured that he would never be called to bear arms against his country.

Hayne was unwilling to sign, but realized that if he refused, it meant prison for him, and he would never see his beloved wife again. He therefore signed. At the same time, however, he wrote to his friend, Doctor David Ramsay, stating that the "signature had been forced upon him by hard necessity," and adding, "I will never bear arms against my countrymen. My masters can require no service of me but what is enjoined by the old militia law of the Province, which substitutes a fine in lieu of personal service. This I will pay for my protection. If my conduct should be censured by my countrymen, I beg that you will remember this conversation and bear witness for me that I do not mean to desert the cause of America."

He was then released and hastened back to his dying wife. After her death, the British continued to harass him. He was ordered to join the army with threat of imprisonment unless he complied. With that, Colonel Hayne felt he was relieved of all obligation of his parole. Being urged by his neighbors and other Charleston patriots to become their leader, he made an open and honorable declaration. He accepted this leadership only on condition that those who served under him would not engage in any conduct of undue severity and that there would be no pillage, nor inhumanity toward the foe. Under those terms, he accepted a rebel commission and raised a company.

Soon afterward he was captured in an engagement and taken to prison in Charles Town. There he was tried for treason. As he was a beloved and influential person, Lord Rawdon had singled him out and determined to sacrifice him as an example. He was declared guilty and condemned to be executed, although it was not stated in what manner this was to be carried out.

When the people learned that a sentence of death had been pronounced, they were stunned. A protest against this injustice came from every quarter, and every possible effort was made to save him. Hayne, himself, had sent a vindication of his conduct and demanded a fair trial. This was ignored.

The ladies of Charles Town, Tory and Whig, got up a petition, professing themeslves "deeply interested and affected by the imminent and shocking doom of the most unfortunate Mr. Hayne," and soliciting its annulment. This, too, was ignored.

A number of loyalist gentlemen interceded for him, and Lieutenant Governor William Bull, who was ill at the time, came on a stretcher to Lord Rawdon to implore a stay of execution.

The more important Hayne became, however, the more decided Rawdon was to use him for his own purposes. He actually thought that by this means he could frighten the people into submission. When, last of all, came the two little sons of Isaac Hayne, with their aunt, Mrs. Peronneau, they were received in the drawing room of the Brewton House which the British lord was occupying. With tears in their eyes, they knelt before him and pleaded that their father's life be spared. But Lord Rawdon's "face gave no grace." According to the official record, he snorted and turned away, dismissing them with a curt grant of a visit to their father only long enough to say good-bye.

The execution day dawned and Colonel Hayne, accompanied by his friends, walked through the streets toward his doom. On this bright morning they walked together for the last time, past familiar scenes, past the people who lined the way in groups, past the house on the corner of Meeting and Atlantic Streets where the faithful Mrs. Peronneau lived.

Mrs. Perroneau, distraught with grief, stood at the north window and saw Colonel Hayne pass.

Overcome with emotion, she cried out to him, "Return— return to us!"

"I will," he called to her, "if I can."

The procession passed in the sunshine on to the gates of King Street with Colonel Hayne as yet anaware of the manner of execution arranged for him.

When he reached the gates and saw the gibbet, his face blanched. He had expected to be shot as a prisoner of war, for hanging was the death meted out to traitors. Nevertheless, his steps did not falter. He mounted the cart—and to a friend who exhorted him to die with courage, he said, "I will try."

For a few moments he prayed with a clergyman, then shook hands solemnly with his friends. Drawing the cap over his face, he himself gave the signal to the hangman.

So passed a noble and courageous man. His death was an example—but not the example that Lord Rawdon intended. On the contrary, it stirred his countrymen to more resolute resistance, and, to freedom.

Did Isaac Hayne return? For almost a hundred years, any-one standing at the north window of the Peronneau House at night could hear his voice in the street. Anyone there after dark could hear his footsteps on the stairs, coming up— always up, as of a man returning.

Only with the rumblings of a new war which set patriot against patriot did his footsteps die away.

The Thirteenth Step

The house was burned many years ago, and only the brick walls remain. An oak tree stands near the empty window in the shell of the northwest room where a bride still mourns the happiness that was snatched from her on her wedding night.

Brick House was built in 1720 and was acquired soon afterward by the Jenkins family. Amelia grew up there with her uncle and aunt. It was a happy childhood, for she and her cousins roamed all over Edisto Island to fish, catch crabs, and swim in the creek.

One of their friends was an Indian boy named Concha, who knew in a special atavistic way the woods and the sea and the birds and the weather. Concha shared in the adventures of the Jenkins children for all those years.

Ammie became a tomboy, managing despite the prescribed long skirts, to climb trees, and to swim, row a boat, ride a horse—she grew up to be a lovely girl, brown and strong like her cousins.

On her eighteenth birthday, Ammie's uncle and aunt gave her the customary party to mark her debut into society. There was great preparation, and the prominent people on the island and from nearby Charles Town were invited. Ammie dressed in great excitement, donning her first evening gown. The dress, with off-the-shoulder bodice, and skirt standing out over hoops and many petticoats, was shining white against the sun-brown of her skin and made Ammie more beautiful than ever. She was pulling on her long white gloves when from outside came a chirping birdcall.

It was Concha—she recognized the call. Many times in the woods they had used it for a signal. But Concha had not been invited to the party. Ammie would have to go and speak to her friend. She hurried down the back steps to find him outside in the garden.

The Indian stared at her. Seeing her in the beautiful dress with the light from the door falling full on her, he blurted out, "Ammie, little flower,—Ammie. I want you. Come, go with Concha, we will know always the woods and the waters and the sky."

"But—" stammered Ammie, "I don't love you like that. You're my friend. I just want to be friends."

"No, no. I want you, little flower, more than anything. More than life."

"Oh, no, Concha. I couldn't."

"Concha not live without Ammie."

"No, stop," and she backed away. "I must go."

"So, Concha waits. Always waits."

Ammie turned and fled to her room, trembling and afraid. But the party was beginning and she was obliged to go downstairs to greet her guests. The disturbing scene with Concha was soon forgotten, for attending the party was Paul Grimball, the most sought-after young man on the island. Recently returned from a trip to Europe, he was attentive only to

Amelia. From that time on they were together constantly, swimming, riding, fishing. They fell deeply in love.

Their engagement was announced. When all the plans were made and the wedding was less than a month away, Amelia was awakened one night by the same birdcall she had heard before. But Amelia did not answer. She had no wish to see Concha.

One day, when Paul was away in Charleston, the skies and the water beckoned, and the restless Amelia decided to go crabbing. Venturing forth alone, she set several lines and was busily wading in the water's edge pulling in crabs, when she suddenly became aware of Concha standing behind her. She was so startled that she slipped and cut her foot on an oyster shell.

Blood colored the water and Ammie turned pale. Concha, murmuring incoherently, took her up in his arms and carried her to a grassy spot under a shady tree. Putting her down, he fell to his knees and, clasping her foot in both hands, cried, "Ammie, Ammie, little flower," and pressed his cheek against her ankle.

"Oh, Concha, it's all right. I must get to the house. Help me, Concha."

But the Indian did not move except to raise his head and look at her.

"Ammie," his voice became hoarse. "Concha not live without you. You not marry with white man."

"I'm sorry, Concha. He is my kind, and I love him."

The Indian stood up, and his face became hard and cruel. "Never, never will Ammie go with other man," he said.

Ammie was feeling sick, and she was suddenly afraid. "Concha," she said, "help me. Take me home. You must take me home."

She began to sob, and the Indian looked at her, hesitating, until she held out her hands to him. He took them and raised her to her feet, but when she swayed uncertainly, he picked her up and carried her in silence, a stern, pained look on his face, his eyes turned away from her.

When they reached the house, he put her on the piazza.

"Never will Ammie go," he said again, "Never!" He walked away into the woods without a sound.

After that, Ammie did not go out alone. Her foot was soon well, and she was full of happiness as her wedding day approached.

On the night before the wedding, when the rehearsal was over, Ammie and Paul slipped away from the guests and went out into the moonlit garden. How beautiful it was! An enchantment seemed cast upon them, so clear and shining was the night. The graceful streamers of moss swayed gently in a stillness broken only by the whisper of the trees. For those two, there was nothing in all the world but themselves and their love. Paul kissed her, and they laughed softly with happiness, promising that they would remember through all the years ahead this night so full of beauty and love and hope. But neither heard the rustle of the leaves in the tree above.

On the wedding night, the hall was filled with family and guests waiting for the bride to come downstairs. Her uncle was there, and the bridegroom watched eagerly for her appearance.

Ammie stood in the northwest bedroom. The veil pinned by the maids on her dark hair fell like a mist about her. She gave a last look in the mirror and was turning to go when from outside came a birdcall. Ammie heard, but she gave no sign. She walked on past the open window with her thoughts on Paul and on her marriage.

Suddenly there was a singing sound—and an arrow struck her breast. At the sharp pain, she uttered a piercing cry.

Swaying unsteadily, she staggered from the room and, reaching the stairs, started down. The guests below watched in horror, seeing the arrow in her side and the red stain spreading on her white gown.

Paul ran to her. He caught her in his arms on the thirteenth step where she collapsed and died.

The thirteenth step. Never, through the years, would any-one put foot on the thirteenth step, for the stain was there—the spot that a century of wear could not wipe out.

And at the northwest window of the fire-gutted house, in the lonely hours of the night, a lady in shimmering white appears. Those who see her hear a birdcall throbbing from the woods, and, at intervals, a ghostly, piercing cry of pain.

VII

Which would be worse? Human fiends or the swamp's terrors?

The Wayfarer

at Six Mile House

It was still and dark that memorable night in 1819. Not a star shone in a sky almost as black as the towering trees under it. It was impossible to see the road which had been cut through swampy underbrush and was at times a foot deep in mud. The only sounds were the pounding of hoofs and the croaking of frogs.

The horse had slowed to a walk after the hard traveling of the afternoon. The wagon she pulled was heavily loaded with hides. John Peeples, who sat huddled on the wagon seat, was tired, too. The reins hung slack in his hands for he had to trust the mare to find the road. The dampness chilled him to the bone. He was uneasy and rode with ears alerted to every sound. *Six Mile House* could not be far away, and he debated whether or not to stop for the night.

At a swooshing noise in the bushes, he almost sprang from his seat—then sank back realizing that it was some big bird rising from its nest. Again all was quiet.

A mournful call trembled on the air—a chuck-will's-widow. He almost wished he had not come. Gruesome tales came to mind: men had mysteriously vanished on this road. And who could tell whether they were victims of human fiends or the evil spirits of the swamp?

His own loss would be keenly felt by his family back in Georgia. At this moment they would be going to bed after praying for his safety—his good wife Bett, Thomas (a big boy now and so helpful), Mary, Johnny, Little Susie, and another soon to be born. It was a fine family. He had been fortunate in picking a wife. She was hard-working and thrifty and had made a good home for them.

In the safety of his cottage, surrounded by his wife and children, it had not seemed possible that some strange mishap might befall him. Even when he was told of the man who had disappeared last month during a journey over this road, he had been unmindful. If a man could not take a chance to better himself, where would he and his folks be? Bound down by poverty, surely. His family had grown, and he had to try to get the best price for his hides. Nowhere was the market so good as in Charleston, and he was set on taking advantage of it.

He smiled remembering how Bett had said, "Don't you be on that road after dark." Well, he had tried. He had urged the mare to all possible speed. Of course, at the last tavern, he had perhaps lingered too long over his mug of ale. Oh, well, tales were only tales after all. There was not necessarily truth in them. In another hour, in Charleston, he would have a good laugh about his fright.

Suddenly, from afar, he saw the twinkle of a tiny light.

"Dear Lord, help me," he thought. "What can this be now? If it's human, it will be robbers and I am lost. Maybe it's some evil thing from the swamp sent to lure me to the devil."

In either case, he was in for trouble. He reached for his knife and placed it on the seat beside him; he was going to put up a fight whatever the unknown offered.

John watched as the light came nearer and grew larger. Soon it was apparent that it came from a window. His heart gave a leap of gladness. This must be the inn! He reached for the reins and flicked them on the horse's back, urging her to a faster pace. At last he would find companionship, a fire, and some ale. At last he would be safe from the horrors of this dark night. The tavern—what luck! There he would stay for the night although he was reluctant to spend the money his frugal wife had saved and provided for just such an emergency. Tomorrow he would push on to the city; the very thought of morning and of Charleston cheered him. He looked forward to making a good sale of his hides and bringing back more than double the money in his wallet which constituted Bett's entire savings during their years together.

He made for the lighted window and soon reached the hitching post where he tied his mare. He went up on the piazza and pushed open the door.

Inside were a cheerful fire on the hearth and laughter, and, behind the bar, was the most beautiful woman he had ever seen. Closing the door after him, he came slowly into the room, staring at the woman in disbelief. She smiled at him, and there was a hint of pleasant satisfaction in her wide velvety eyes.

"Good e'en, Traveler," she said. "Welcome to *Six Mile House*."

She threw back her head and from her lips came a jeering laugh that to John was more fearful than the black night outside.

There were men, too, a tall one named John Fisher and one called Hayward, along with several others. They all turned to stare at him and, grinning, bade him welcome. They actually seemed overly friendly; one went to put up his horse and run the wagon into the barn. There was much good humor and questioning as he drank his ale, and the woman served him a meal of stew and bread. When his hunger was satisfied, they suggested a game of chance.

Peeples was wary. He was not of a mind to lose Bett's savings to a gang of card sharks; he pleaded weariness and a countryman's habit of retiring early. So, with much jollity and many guffaws, the group escorted him to sleeping quarters behind the taproom.

John was far from the simple rustic he pretended to be. He did not like the looks of this company including the woman with her impudent beauty and wild laughter. He had noticed the meaningful glances exchanged between her and one of the men. Recollecting the tales of foul play he had heard, he knew that it would be as easy to dispose of him here as upon the lonely road. He wished now that he had not heeded the beckoning light but had chosen to brave the terrors of the dark.

Scratching his head, he weighed his chances. It would be foolish to try to escape now. He must think of some plan to use later. Perhaps when they went to sleep—if they did—or if they left only one to watch the door, he would stand a better chance. There was the window—but he must wait until all was quiet so that he could get the horse and his hides.

Finally he hit upon a plan. Taking some of the bed clothes and a pillow, he made a dummy and covered it on the bed. Then removing half of his money from the wallet, he put it in his pocket and placed the wallet on the chair beside the bed. Blowing out the lantern, he sat down behind a stand in the dark corner to wait until it was safe to go.

Soon, weary from his traveling, he slept. How much time passed he could not tell, but he waked to hear a low murmur of voices. Light came from a slit in the wall, and he stole over to peer through the crack into the bright taproom. There he saw the man named Fisher and the woman seated at a table counting the coins from his wallet.

The man pushed the money aside in disgust, "Scarcely enough," he said, "to pay his board."

"But the wagon," whispered his wife. "It is full of hides. Aye, ye will realize a goodly sum for that."

The man puckered his mouth and nodded his head. He was well-pleased over that.

The woman spoke again, "I will attend to him at breakfast."

Peeples stared at her, thinking, "Oh, no, my beauty. I will be on my way long before a poisoned breakfast!"

And he heard the man say, "We'll turn him in now and go to sleep."

She clutched at his arm, "No—John, leave him to me. I can't listen to his cries down there for all the time that it takes to die."

Fisher pushed her away and strode over to the wall. She followed, clinging to him.

Throwing her from him so violently that she fell to the floor, he reached up and grasped with both hands an iron handle and, straining and pulling, managed to force it all the way to the floor.

A creaking and scraping sound followed. Suddenly there was a great rushing noise behind Peeples. When he turned his head, what he saw made his knees buckle, and he clung to the wall for support. There where he had placed the dummy was no bed—no floor. There was only a great gaping hole! And had he, himself, stretched out his tired body between the sheets, his cries would even now be heard—and for as long as it takes to die.

He looked down where the streak of light fell into the dark pit and saw the gleam of something white. Bones. Human bones! Skeletons, no doubt, of other wayfarers like himself. Almost paralyzed with horror and fright, he yet had one clear thought: he must get away at once if he hoped to live.

He ran to the window, his bare feet making no noise on the planks of the floor. Springing from the sill, he landed on his feet outside and made for the stable. It was unlocked, "God be thanked," and there was his horse. He swung himself on her back and, clinging to her mane, kicked his heels into her sides, praying—all the time praying—that she would respond.

The good beast seemed to understand. She threw up her head and raced for the open road. How welcome now were the darkness and the hoarse cries of the frogs!

There was shouting behind, for his escape was immediately discovered. Two musket shots went by his head, but Peeples did not slow his pace. He kept his head down, his arms clasped around the horse's neck. He had a good start, and he urged his mare on as though a demon were after him. He knew now how men disappeared. No more stops at taverns for him! Passing *Four Mile House* on the run, he pressed on to Charleston.

Next morning he told his tale to the authorities who listened attentively. At last they had proof. This was no vague rumor of a crime; this was attempted murder, and now the law could take a hand. The sheriff's deputy and a party of gentlemen set out to capture the gang and bring them in to Charleston.

Lavinia Fisher and her husband, John, were taken with five of their accomplices and lodged in jail. The trial record of 1819 tells that "two bodies were dug up, which was enough to condemn them." The rest of the story was suppressed, but many knew about the skeletons in the cellar and told their children and their children's children. It became a legend, and the burning of *Six Mile House* could not hush the matter up.

The murderers were found guilty and sentenced to be hanged. Velvety-eyed Lavinia, dressed in her wedding clothes, and hoping to the end her sultry beauty would save her, was executed before a great crowd. The gallows was set up on the Meeting Street Road where the Cooper River Bridge traffic now enters it.

At the last Lavinia stood on the platform and cried, "If ye have a message ye want to send to Hell, give it to me—I'll carry it!"

Six Mile House stood where the Old Dorchester Road crossed the Goose Creek Road at Ashley Ferry. One of these roads led to the upper part of the state and the other into Georgia.

Four Mile House still stands, for it was run by reputable people. It is often pointed out as the scene of the wayfarer crimes. This is not so. The Fisher trial record mentions the burning of *Six Mile House* where the murders took place. Its scorched ruins remained for years beside the new inn that was built to replace it.

No one has ever heard where Lavinia and John Fisher came from, nor even of anyone remotely related to them. In Charleston, the woman's legendary beauty has grown with the years.

The Passenger

from Cuckols Creek

O ne winter night, Mr. Heyward, a plantation owner, and Mr. Jaycocks, his overseer, were going to meet the train at White Hall Station. Its arrival was anticipated with much pleasure for Mr. Heyward's brother, Izard, was coming for a visit.

After driving for miles, they came to Cuckols Creek which bordered the rice plantation's southern limits. Mr. Jaycocks drew in the reins to slow down the horse for the creek crossing. But the horse shied at the wooden bridge and the driver had trouble holding him to the road.

"You know, Mr. Heyward, not a darkie will come near this spot after dark," said the overseer. "They say there is a 'hant' here."

"Is that so?" said Mr. Heyward. "What happens?"

"Not a one will say. They shake their heads and mumble."

Mr. Heyward laughed. "I don't see any spook, do you?"

"No, Sir, and I hope I don't."

They drove on and soon reached the lights of White Hall Station where they did not have long to wait.

After hearty greetings were exchanged, Brother Izard was put into the back seat of the surrey with his baggage. Mr. Heyward rode up front with Mr. Jaycocks, who continued to drive. However, the horse needed no guidance, knowing well the familiar road. A quarter-moon hung in the sky, and the night was clear and cool.

Brother Izard started in to talk. After years of absence, he was returning to the old home, and he loved the place, the family, and its traditions. And although he frequently used the ejaculation "Eh?" and although he asked many questions, he gave no one a chance to answer, for every question brought some recollection which started another line of reminiscing.

Up front, his brother and Mr. Jaycocks listened with amusement, nodding and chuckling, and at times bursting into loud guffaws.

"Well, well," said Izard. "I will be glad to see the old place again. Haven't been there since I was a boy. *The Swamp,* eh? Not a pretty name for it, but better at that than *Amsterdam.* Crazy notion the old man took after his European trip, to name his plantations after cities in Holland and Germany. *Rotterdam,* mind you, and *Hamburg.* Too fancy for the Negroes, eh? They stuck to *'de Swamp.'* "

Mr. Heyward started to speak—but brother Izard was declaring, "Old Nathaniel was a great boy—eighty-six years in this old world and sixty of them spent right here as a planter. And the dickens of a successful one—at rice, too—hurricanes or no hurricanes, and every day he drove over the place, from the creek all the way to the river. The creek was his biggest worry—to keep the water back in a freshet, eh?"

Again Mr. Heyward opened his mouth to comment, and again could not be heard.

His brother went on, "He was old in that portrait of him, but his eyes are bright, and they seem to look straight through you. And what a determined set to his jaw! He was so old that his hair was wispy and white, but a lovable codger he must have been."

"Yes, I—"

"Remember the story of the time he was ill? And Dr. Ozier came from Charleston in a steamboat? He got here at night, and next day when they put the old man in the boat to take him to the city, the darkies, who had never seen a boat like that, ran along the bank crying, 'Oh, me Gawd. Oh, me Gawd. De devil got ole Maussuh.'"

At Cuckols Creek, the horse slowed to cross the bridge. Loose planks rattled loudly under the carriage wheels. Once more the mare began to prance and started off at a brisker pace than before, her ears alert and her nostrils quivering.

Suddenly all became quiet. There was not a sound save the muffled clop of the hoofs on the soft earth. Mr. Heyward turned in surprise to look at his brother and saw him apparently wrapped in thought and staring straight ahead. He ventured to remark that they were having a fair spell of weather.

No answer.

He said that the rice crop this year had been a good one.

No comment.

He told Izard that old Cudjo would be overjoyed to see him, and Scipio, and Maum Sarah.

Still, not a word.

Mr. Heyward and Mr. Jaycocks looked at each other, puzzled. They shrugged and turned their eyes to the road as the carriage jogged along in silence.

There was an eerie soundlessness over the countryside as they passed from marshland to wooded spaces, where gray moss hung cadaverously from bare tree limbs; then on to open stretches where the Combahee River shone palely against the blackness of bordering grasses.

A flock of ducks crossed in the path of the moon, the weird swishing of their wings breaking the stillnesss. Bushes and twisted tree trunks took on strange shapes and seemed to move like furtive shadows. The monotonous rhythm of the hoofbeats was like the summons of a phantom drum.

A cold sensation crept up Mr. Heyward's spine and he turned to ask anxiously, "Are you all right, Izard?"

Forthcoming from the rear was no sign nor sound.

Mr. Heyward shook his head and turned back. He, too, now, stared ahead in awful uncertainty.

For miles they traveled thus, and all the while the horse raced, her ears twitching nervously. At last they drew up to the steps of the house.

Mr. Heyward sprang out of the surrey and approached his brother. He was deeply worried.

"I say, Izard. Are you all right?"

"Yes—yes, Clinch. I am."

"What was the matter? I never knew you to stop talking."

"Well, I'll tell you," said his brother. "When we crossed the creek, a man got in the carriage and sat on the seat beside me. I didn't know who he was, but he liked me, and I liked him. We were happy riding along together and if I had spoken, it might have spoiled it, see? And I didn't want him to go. But when we stopped—he wasn't there."

"Great Heavens, Man! You saw the ghost."

"Well I'll be—. That hair so wispy and white, and those piercing eyes, and the firmly set jaw. I'll be damned if it wasn't Old Nathaniel himself!"

The Leaning Tombstone

G hosts?" Sallie's scornful laughter rang out in the spacious hallway. "Surely you don't believe in ghosts?"

The house between St. Philip's and the Huguenot church was built, like most old Charleston houses, with a spacious hall on the first floor and a large reception room used for private dances on the second floor. At the foot of the great stairway, Sallie and her friends had lingered to talk after supper, knowing that the orchestra would not yet be ready to resume playing.

Sallie stood on the first step, with the frilled train of her gown making an island at her feet. Her shoulders were bare except for the dark curl and red rose that lay upon her neck. Sallie was popular. Most of the young men at the ball were captivated by her flirtatious glances and her rippling infectious laughter. But Sallie had, besides, beauty and much sweetness.

Her friend Alice said, "When we passed St. Philip's grave-yard tonight, the horses shied. I was frightened half out of my wits."

Another said, "It's so dark and spooky in there, and there *is* a ghost, you know."

"Don't you believe in ghosts, Sallie?" asked Alice.

"Certainly not," declared Sallie, tossing her curls. "Darkies talk about ghosts, but have you ever known anyone who has seen one?"

"I have heard—"

"Yes," Sallie interrupted, "you have heard. But you have never seen."

"A ghost does walk that graveyard," Alice insisted. "Maum Delia says Old Peter saw it, just before he died."

"Old Peter dreamed it—or his old eyes played tricks on him."

Alice raised her voice, "It's a gray man, and he stands by old Mr. Smith's tombstone. You know, it's the tallest one, that leans to one side."

"It's a shadow, most likely," declared Sallie.

"Oh, no! Maum Delia says that if you see him, you are go-ing to die."

"I would prefer not to go there after dark," said someone.

"So would I," said Ben gruffly.

"Why?" Sallie turned to him. "What is there to be afraid of?"

He shrugged. "I'd rather not go, that's all."

A friend came to the rescue. "Come, Sallie, you wouldn't go there either, you know," he said.

"Of course I would," Sallie insisted.

"I don't believe it."

"Nor I."

Sallie's temper flared. "But I would," she said. "Don't be silly!"

Alice cried, "We dare you then."

"Dare?"

"Yes. We dare you to go to the graveyard alone."

"All right, I'll go," said Sallie. She took a step down and started for the door.

They laughed lightly, not taking her seriously until she said, "You will wait for me here?"

"Don't let them tease you, Miss Sallie," Ben said. "Let's go upstairs. The dancing will begin again in a minute."

But one young man had already gone to the hall closet and was returning with a walking cane. "Here," he said. "Take this and plant it in the ground by the leaning stone. Then we will know that you really got that far."

"Very well," said the girl and, taking the cane, walked out of the front door, not heeding Ben's plea to come back and scorning his offer to accompany her. "No, Ben, I am not afraid. Really! What could happen to me?"

Excitement with overtones of fear gripped the group. Ben stepped out of the door and stood on the sidewalk, staring after Sallie as she walked determinedly, with her head high, and her long skirt trailing and sweeping the bricks of the uneven paving. The others crowded around the doorway. It was the last time her friends—including Ben, who loved her—would ever see Sallie alive.

The stillness of midnight hovered over the deserted street. The light on the lamp post flickered, making jumping shadows. There was a half-moon and the columns of St. Philip's showed dimly; the outline of the steeple was hazy in the night. Across the street from the church were the iron fence of the graveyard and the tall iron gates. Inside was complete darkness.

Ben saw Sallie push open the gate and took a step to follow; but a storm of protest stopped him.

Sallie went through the gate and disappeared from view as the darkness closed about her.

Until then Sallie had not been afraid. But on the far side of the fence she felt she would be smothered by the clutching shadows and the tombstones' menacing shapes. The dim moon-light weirdly speckled the ground before her but in the far reaches of the graveyard loomed a terrifying blackness. She hurried, scorning her sense of uneasiness, and searched blindly for the leaning stone.

A rustle in the leaves made her heart beat wildly. Sallie wished that she had not been so foolhardy, but her pride drove her on. This was a dare, and with Sallie a dare was no light thing.

A dog howled in the distance. At the almost human sound, Sallie's lips trembled. She was shaking, but she stumbled on, gripping the walking cane until at last she came to the end of the graveyard, and the moonbeams dimly revealed the leaning tombstone.

Rushing to it, she touched the cold marble. Then she turned to run but remembered the cane and stopped. She looked behind her and what she saw glazed her eyes with horror. With a swift jerk, she stabbed the cane blindly into the ground and, clutching her skirts, tried to lift her train so she could flee—.

But, she could not move.

Sallie was held firmly to the spot, surrounded by the beckoning tombstones and the creeping shadows. Her blood had turned to ice in her veins. She threw back her head and tried to scream, but no sound came from her paralyzed throat. She sank to the ground, unconscious.

At the house, her friends, standing in the brightly lighted hall, talked uneasily in broken sentences, their eyes searching the open door for Sallie's return. Ben paced outside in frenzied anxiety.

As time wore on, they looked at each other with increasing fearfulness. Finally Alice voiced what all were thinking: "You know she should be back by now!"

They rushed to the street and, seeing no one, broke into a run, with Ben out in front.

They dashed across the street, opened the gate, and thronged into the silent, lonely graveyard. There they found her, beside the leaning tombstone, dead—the frills of her train pinned securely to the ground by the deeply imbedded walking cane.

And now Sallie's ghost returns to the spot where her proud heart failed—lovely Sallie with her fluttering frills and the rose in her hair.

FENWICK HALL

"Ann loved the house and all its mysteries."

The Legend of Fenwick Castle

Ann Fenwick opened her eyes with a start remembering this was a special day. Springing from her bed, she ran to the window. Below was her mother's sunken garden and beyond, the great forest where the sun was struggling to get through the branches of the large trees to the new spring growth beneath. The jasmine, in full bloom, made yellow designs in the garden and filled the air with its fragrance. But the sun was much higher than she wished, for this was to be the most exciting day of all her seventeen years.

The night before, her father had told her that among the horses arriving from England at dawn would be a thoroughbred racer, the finest to be bought. And nothing could please Ann more than a beautiful horse. This love had been instilled in her from earliest childhood by her father, whose favorite she was. Edward Fenwick was feared by many for his stern, demanding ways, but with his daughter he had always been gentle and indulgent.

She was thinking of him now as she hurried into her clothes, wondering if he were already out looking at the horses. She was sure he would be, for nothing that happened at Fenwick escaped his interest and personal direction.

Dressed at last, she ran down the long stairway. In the downstairs hall she passed the familiar suit of armor, and the old sea chest which always brought to mind her forbidding Great-Uncle Robert. He had died long before she was born, but the slaves had used his fearsome imaginary presence to frighten her: Great-Uncle Robert of the evil dark eyes, the swarthy cheeks, the flourishing mustaches. Whenever he had been at Fenwick, mysterious things had happened, such as the hauling in of big chests brought by boats on the Stono River. The chests had been stored in the big room in the basement, which had a small tunnel leading toward the Stono—so that Uncle Robert could get away if the "law" came, the slaves said. Her father had once let her look down the dark narrow passageway which had smelled damp and musty. Of course, it was fascinating to have a pirate—even a dead one—among one's kith and kin, but it was hard to believe that anybody in her own father's family could have been so wicked and ruthless.

Outside the house, Ann paused to look up at the imposing mansion. Some people thought it strange that her grandfather had wanted to build there on John's Island. But what more beautiful spot could he have found? Besides, what John Fenwick had most wanted was a castle like the family place in England where the title of Lord Ripon had come to him. Fenwick did remind one of a castle now that Edward Fenwick, Ann's father, had added two-story brick extensions at the sides. And there was a secret stairway behind the great chimney. Ann loved the house and all its mysteries.

Even more than the house, though, she loved the fine horses her father imported. Crossing at the back to the stable yard, her eyes searched among the many excellent steeds. Ah, there was the new thoroughbred, sleek and black and poised—there was no mistaking him! Radiant with excitement, she ran over to him but refrained from touching him for he was strange and nervous. She stood appraising the animal until she noticed the groom standing at the horse's head. He was young and handsome, and she liked his eyes when he turned to her.

"Oh," Ann finally said. "And this is the new thoroughbred?"

"Yes, Miss." His steady gaze held her own.

"What is his name?"

"Sultan, Miss."

"Oh." She saw the horse, but she was looking at the groom when she added, "He's beautiful."

"Yes, Miss." He went on staring at her as though he had never seen her like before.

Her father came up. Neither was aware of his presence until he said, "Take him away, Tony. Give him a rubdown."

Ann stood and watched the horse and groom leave the yard before she turned and went back into the house. She ate her breakfast with a faraway, dreamy look in her eyes and a wistful smile on her lips.

Every day when Ann rode, as was her custom, a groom accompanied her. She began to request regularly that Tony be assigned to this duty. They took long rides together and when they were far from the house, would talk about their families and the horses and anything at all until finally there grew between them an understanding so deep that sometimes, for long periods at a time, words were unnecessary. Soon they realized that only when they were together were they happy.

Ann was sure of the thing she wanted more than anything else in the world when she went to her father one morning. She asked his permission for her to marry Tony.

But Lord Ripon stared at her with disbelief. "You cannot mean it!" he said. "My daughter marry a groom? You are out of your mind!"

Ann was quietly determined. "He is not just a groom, Papa. He is the son of a clergyman who came to this country like so many younger sons of noblemen to make his own way. You could help Tony to get established in some honorable profession."

Lord Ripon was losing his temper. "Never, I tell you! Never will I give my consent to such a marriage. A groom—a common horse tender who tells you fine stories. Never! I would rather see you in your grave."

Afterward the couple could no longer ride together openly but had to meet secretly.

When Ann told Tony her father would not consent to their marriage, he offered to make the next overture to Lord Ripon.

"No—no, I will try once more," said Ann, breaking away reluctantly from the shelter of Tony's arms.

But it was weeks before despair gave her the courage to face her father again.

"Never!" her father answered the new plea.

"But, I beg you—" Ann insisted.

"Never, I told you!" her father shouted. "Don't speak to me of it again."

Without hope, Ann sought out Tony at their secret meeting place near a stream hidden from the house by a copse of pine. He was as undismayed at the new development as the brook flowing merrily over the rocks.

"We shall go away and be married then!" he said. "And there will be nothing your father can do about it!"

Ann agreed, and they made their plans. The first day Lord Ripon went to the city, Ann and Tony rode away together through the autumn woods. They found a minister and were married. By nightfall they had reached the marshes of the Ashley river and in the distance could see across the water the houses of Charles Town. There was no boat in which to make the crossing; they would have to wait for morning when they could obtain passage with some city-bound traveler.

Back in a clearing was a deserted log cabin. They decided to stay there for the night. Tying their horses to a tree, they stood and watched the pale of evening change to darkness.

Above were the stars; below was the lapping of the water; and before them was one night of happiness.

With the dawn came the clatter of horses' hoofs and the rumble of coach wheels. Lord Ripon had found them.

A loud and angry voice ordered them to come out.

When Tony opened the door, he was seized by several men. He struggled, but they bound his arms behind him and forced him into the waiting coach. Ann's father pushed her in behind him and slammed the door.

During the long journey back to Fenwick they rode in silence. Ann, with her head on Tony's shoulder, trembled and did not dare to speak. She knew her father's anger would be terrible, but mercifully, neither she nor Tony could envision what awaited them at the end of that ride.

Into the stable yard the coach went and drew to a stop beneath the great oak. When the door was opened, Ann stepped out to face her father.

"I am Tony's wife," she said almost defiantly. "The Reverend Mr. Marshall married us yesterday."

Lord Ripon's face was red with rage. "Get him out," he roared. "Seat him on a horse."

Ann rushed to her father. She threw herself against him crying, "Papa, no—no! He is my husband. I love him!"

Pushing her aside, he shouted to his men, "Now, the rope. Put it around his neck—bind it to the limb of the oak."

Ann watched in horror. Clinging to her father's arm, she sobbed, "No—no—no—."

Her father answered her entreaties by taking a whip and forcing it into her hand. Then, holding her, he made her lunge forward and strike the horse.

The surprised animal sprang away, leaving its rider dangling in the air—twisting, turning, from side to side.

Ann screamed her husband's name before she collapsed. She was carried unconscious to the house.

When she revived, she called for Tony, asking where he was, begging him to come to her. Her mother and the slaves caring for her tried to tell her what had happened, but she would not believe it. She got up and started searching through the house, in and out of the rooms, day and night, never resting, calling, "Tony—Tony!"

The years passed with Ann sitting at times in the east parlor staring into space or wandering through the rooms, up and down the stairs, searching and calling, "Tony, where are you, Tony?"

Her hair turned white and her skin became grayed and wrinkled with age. Still her east parlor vigil and her search continued until death came at last to end them.

And yet they were not finished, for Ann searches still at *Fenwick Castle*. Her footsteps as she passes through the halls and up and down the stairs are always accompanied by the mournful call, "Tony—Tony—Tony!"

Edward Fenwick was a loyalist and at the Revolution's onset fled to New York where he died in 1775. Eventually another family lived at *Fenwick Castle* in luxury and elegance until another war destroyed all means of subsistence. The house, with the race course and garden fell prey to neglect. For many years it remained a haunted ruin, feared and shunned by all.

Recently restored, *Fenwick Hall* is now one of the show places of the Low Country. When the new owner was planning its redecoration, she had a photograph made of the mantel in the east parlor. The picture faithfully reproduced the room features in every detail and showed, in the fireplace, a gibbet with a body hanging from it—the same vision so grievously impressed upon the mind and heart of Ann Fenwick.

The Ghost of Daughter Dale

I wish there *were* a ghost," the lady said. She had recently acquired an old house on Church Street, and was showing it to her daughter who had come to visit her.

"It was built before 1733 and at that time was outside the walls of the town. An old deed records that Colonel Miles Brewton 'conveyed' it 'for love and affection to daughter Dale, wife of Dr. Thomas Dale.'

"You see how thick the walls are," the lady continued. "The brick, called 'rose brick' was brought over from England as ballast. The house is old enough to have a ghost."

From room to room they went, starting at the front door, which opened on the living room. From the dining room which came next, there were quaint steps leading to the floor above. Upstairs were three rooms at the front and two at the back. Yet from the exterior it appeared a very small house.

"It was originally three stories high," the owner explained, "but a hundred years ago, someone saw fit to take off the upper story. Otherwise it is unchanged although it was once used as a storehouse and in later years as a butcher shop. I am lucky to have been able to get it. Only—I wish it had a ghost!"

The daughter was amused and at bedtime retired in a happy frame of mind. She occupied the middle room on the front which was completely shut off from the sea breeze by the close walls of the house next door. It was oppresssively hot and the room was bright with moonlight.

She found it impossible to go to sleep and tossed for hours, thinking about everything but a ghost.

"And then," she tells it, "I saw a woman enter the room from the door across the room. She wore a tight basque and full skirt, and in her arms she carried a baby. I was startled, wondering who could be coming into the room at that hour. I saw her quite distinctly and watched her come across to me and stand at the foot of the bed.

"Then—she vanished. And there followed a horrible sensation. The place was filled with a sort of vibration, and I wanted to cry out. Reaching frantically for the electric switch, I flooded the room with light. But, even in the light, the vision and the horror remained, and I spent long miserable hours waiting for the dawn."

When breakfast time came at last, she drank her coffee gratefully, listening to her mother's gay chatter. When her mother said once more, "I *wish* I had a ghost," the daughter put down her cup and looked at her.

"Mother," she said. "You *have* a ghost."

There were no questions asked. Mother moved out next day and never went back.

What tragedy, I wondered, what sorrow came to this house, that a ghost must linger, forever dwelling with its unhappiness? Could it be Daughter Dale? Her story no one knows. It is lost in the passing of two centuries.

There are on record, however, some interesting facts about

her husband, Dr. Thomas Dale. Besides being a doctor of medicine, he was an assistant justice. McCrady, in his *History of South Carolina,* notes that "Chief Justice Wright complains to the Board of Trade in 1733 of an act impowering the Governor to nominate assistant justices and that under it Governor Johnson had granted commissions to Thomas Dale and Thomas Lamboll, persons entirely ignorant of the law, who assumed to overrule him whenever they thought proper."

McCrady also states that "assistant justices served without pay or emolument of any kind, simply for the honor of the position."

Dr. Dale wrote the first American epilogue known to be signed by its author. It was spoken at the performance of the "Recruiting Officer," the first play to be given at the Dock Street Theatre in 1736. It was later printed in *The Gentleman's Magazine,* London. Seven lines of it so scandalized Miss Eola Willis that she omitted them from her book, *The Charleston Stage in the Eighteenth Century.*

The talented Dr. Dale was popular—undoubtedly so, with the ladies. Was he an individual who gave unhappiness to a loving young wife? Did he, as he says in his epilogue,

> With scandal and quadrille address the dames;
> And strut the fair ones into wanton flames?

Here Miss Willis cut the poem. She writes that "not being furnished with 'vizards' [masks], we have done the best we could."

Dr. Dale records that he "ne'er wrote before or ne'er wrote epilogue." Thus, he was an assistant justice who knew no law and a poet who had never written a poem, but he lives on in the historical records of Charleston. No one knows anything about his wife except that her father gave her the Church Street house; yet her ghost lingers there, where evidently she knew lasting sorrow.

*With ghostly persuasion, an
Irish governess finds piety*

Mary Hyrne Protests

The day was fair and mild. A haze hung upon the sea, paling the distant outline of the shore. The ship, after months of rough weather, was at last making port under full sail. She bobbed gently with the lapping of the water against her prow and bore steadily on, past the many islands and into the harbor of Charleston.

On the bow stood a woman, slight and tall. Becomingly garbed in a red cloak and bonnet, she held to the stays of the ship as her skirts blew in the breeze. She watched the shore line become trees and houses, and in their midst against the sky rose the shining outline of a steeple.

This was the far country she had come to seek. Leaving behind all she knew or cared for, Mrs. Latham had set out to seek employment in a new world. Widowed and without means of support, she had listened to the extraordinary tales of this land of opportunity and with hope in her heart, finally set sail from her native Ireland.

It was not only employment that Mrs. Latham wished to find. Her secret yearning was for romance. She was young and her marriage to Mr. Latham had been one of expediency; now she wished ardently to find a consuming love such as those in the novels that she so avidly read.

Once ashore, she lost no time in taking her letters to the authorities and was gratified to learn that a place could be found for her immediately. She was to set out the next day for *Old Goose Creek Plantation,* where she would teach four little girls.

Her bags and boxes were piled on top of the post chaise sent for her, and she sat in the comfortably padded interior. The coachman got up on the box, flicked the reins on his horses' backs, and they were off.

The scenery was delightful. Mrs. Latham had never before seen trees hung with moss. The long stretches of woods were followed unexpectedly by open spaces where the sunshine sparkled on the blue waters of the creek, and the haze made lavender tones in the tawny golds of the marshes. It was all new and strange and exciting.

Upon arrival she was greeted by Mrs. Henry Smith and her small daughters. The little girls hung back shyly, staring in disbelief at their new governess. They found her young and pretty and gay; they liked her red cloak and her beribboned bonnet, and they were won completely by her sweet smile.

Mrs. Smith said, "You will occupy the west room upstairs. Since my husband's death, the girls and I have moved down to the first floor, but, if you wish, I will have one of the servants sleep up there so you won't be all alone."

"Oh, really, Madam, I will not be afraid to stay up there. What could possibly happen to me? I beg you, don't give it a thought."

Mrs. Latham moved in with her possessions—her clothes, several textbooks, and a few novels she had brought with her to beguile her spare time and to gratify her interest in romance. She felt happy in her cheery, big, high-ceilinged bedroom, with its tall windows overlooking the blue waters where they curved around a point of land and gave the place its name of Goose Creek.

The next morning was Sunday. The family assembled in the hall downstairs for devotions; the servants gathered on the back piazza, where it was customary to have the service read to them. Mrs. Latham stayed in her room to read *The Turkish Spy*.

The quiet of the religious hour was suddenly broken by the sound of hasty footsteps overhead and the appearance of Mrs. Latham on the stairway, wide-eyed and trembling. She cried out hysterically, "Who was that who just went out?"

Mrs. Smith and the children regarded her with amazement. No one had passed. When Mrs. Latham was unconvinced, she was told it was not possible for anyone to leave the house without going through the hall and no one had gone that way.

Then followed much confusion as both services were abandoned and everyone joined in the search for the mysterious person.

No one was found.

Mrs. Latham then related her experience. She had been sitting in her room, reading the novel, when she heard a commotion in the hall outside. She put down her book and listened attentively, as the footsteps came up to her door.

She said, "The door opened slowly, and there stood an old lady. She wore a black gown and a muslin neckerchief crossed on her breast; on her head was a close-fitting white cap. I arose, puzzled, because no one had mentioned any other occupant of the house, and asked her politely, 'Will you come in?' She stared at me and did not say a word. Again I said, 'Come in, won't you?'

"There was still no answer, only a disapproving glare. So I went toward her, holding out my hand, and she moved slowly off.

"A cold draught seemed to fill the room. I was repelled, and at the same time attracted, incredibly attracted to her. I followed, drawn by this force, as she glided with a strange smoothness, always several paces ahead, into the next room and on into the smaller room beyond. From there I knew she could not escape. But—there she vanished.

"I turned and ran back through all the rooms, thinking I must have missed her, that surely she was hiding. But she was gone!"

It was some time before they could pacify Mrs. Latham, or comfort her. She was not convinced by their assurances and she knew she was not mistaken. She accepted gratefully the offer to have someone sleep upstairs.

The following Sunday, Mr. Benjamin Smith came to visit his brother's widow.

At sight of him, the governess again became hysterical crying out, "You are like her. Heaven help me, you are the living image of the old lady who glared at me!"

It was only after talking to her at some length that Mr. Smith calmed her fears.

"My mother, Mary Hyrne, spent the last years of her life in these rooms upstairs," he told her. "She seldom came down, and it was customary for the family to take their work or books up there to sit with her. She was a dear old lady and kind. In the closet of one room she had many little partitions built, in which she kept sugar dainties for her small grandchildren."

Mr. Smith then intimated that perhaps his mother, who was a very pious woman, was displeased with Mrs. Latham for reading a novel on the Sabbath instead of attending the religious service with the family. She was no doubt concerned about the influence Mrs. Latham might have upon the minds of her granddaughters and had come back to protest.

This advice had a remarkable effect upon the Irishwoman. From that day on, she became a faithful and pious governess. She did find romance, for she married again and lived to teach four generations of Smiths and many children of other distinguished Charleston families. She always delighted in telling her "Phantom Story."

Of recent years, on the site of the ruins of *Goose Creek Plantation*, the "Yeamans' Hall" development of handsome winter homes has been built. A central clubhouse was erected for the diversion of the homeowners, and some Charleston ladies one day were assisting in its decoration. One of the party, separated from the others for a short time, was puzzled to see an old lady come into the room, pause, stare, and then go away.

"It was an old lady in an old-fashioned black dress with a muslin neckerchief, and she had on a little white cap," she said. "Who else is here with us?"

She was told, in a voice full of respect, "It was Mary Hyrne —protesting again."

The Fateful Handkerchief

Suppose he doesn't come!" The bride's sister held her lace fan to her lips as she whispered to her cousin. Her eyes anxiously searched the entrance to the room.

Among the many wedding guests discoursing gaily in the handsome home of Rawlins Lowndes, she alone was disturbed. The others did not know what she knew.

"Who doesn't come?" The cousin drew nearer with sudden interest.

There was no reply, only the same anxious peering.

The cousin, determined now to find out, persisted, "What are you trying to tell me?"

Finally the answer came, hesitantly, "They had a quarrel, a really dreadful quarrel."

"But surely that would not keep him from coming!"

"One never knows," the sister shrugged. "He was here yesterday, all excited, demanding to see Ruth. They talked behind closed doors. Something about a handkerchief, of all things! He left in a great rage. Never have I seen a man so angry."

"Pooh, a lover's quarrel. He certainly would not offer insult to Rawlins over so trifling a matter."

"Ruth is nervous. She is terribly afraid, if you ask me."

"Francis Simmons is a man of honor," said the cousin. "He will come."

In a room that opened off the back hall, the stringed orchestra played soft music. The air was faintly perfumed by gardenias that banked the marble mantels. Countless wax tapers in crystal chandeliers and in candlesticks shed a diffused light upon the distinguished gathering. The ladies wore muslin or satin, fashioned in the Empire style after the prevailing French mode. The gentlemen were in richly colored coats with brass buttons and smoothly fitting breeches. Their high pointed collars were bound in white stocks that finished in a tie in front.

One guest whispered to another, "I didn't expect this wedding, did you?"

The other shook her head, "I didn't think that she would get him. They were not together at the Jockey Club Ball."

"Nor at the St. Cecilia. He was all eyes for the Smith girl."

"One never knows. Ruth has a way of getting what she wants."

"Where is Sabina tonight? I thought she was Ruth's closest friend."

"Someone said she was ill and could not come."

"Really?"

There was a stir among the guests, and all turned to see the young Mrs. Lowndes come in. Stepmother of the bride, and scarcely three years her senior, she was pretty and fresh-looking with dark eyes and bright cheeks. She took her place near the improvised altar and waited for the bride to make her entrance.

Next came the Bishop. The anxious sister still peering at the door, saw two men behind him.

"Thank Heavens, there he is! Francis has come!" she whispered. His friend, Henry Deas, was at his elbow and seemed to propel him into the room. The groom had a determined set to his mouth, but he walked as if in a trance. Heedless of the people, and staring above their heads, he came like a man going to his execution. Nor did he give any sign of recognition when his bride appeared.

A charming picture she made, this doll-like person, with big blue eyes. Her muslin dress was embroidered elaborately and finished with handmade lace at neck and sleeves. A short veil, held by tiny clusters of orange blossoms, covered her face. With her was her distinguished father, a man of sixty-five years.

So happy was Ruth to see Francis that she raised her eyes to look directly at him through the veil, seeking some show of attention. Her heart quickened to see how handsome he was in his plum coat and white satin breeches. His chin was primly set between the points of his high collar.

He refused to acknowledge her glance and remained coolly indifferent.

When Mr. Lowndes extended his daughter's hand, as the ceremony required, the groom's hand closed over hers impersonally. By no gesture did he show any awareness of his bride. Like an automaton he stood beside her and repeated the words spoken by the Bishop.

After the service, the couple turned to greet the wedding guests, and few failed to notice that the groom did not kiss his bride.

The brilliant reception was undimmed, however. Witty conversation and bright laughter filled the rooms. Flirtations, brilliant repartee, and happiness were everywhere, it seemed, except in the heart of the groom. At his side the bride shone joyous and triumphant as the slaves, with unfailing good humor, served the food and replenished the gentlemen's glasses with Madiera and rum punch.

At last it was over. The gay throng departed, the candles were snuffed, the last good night said. The bridegroom helped his bride into the yellow, gilt-trimmed coach he had recently had made for her. A coachman sat upon the box and a footman rode behind.

Francis got in beside Ruth on the narrow seat padded with brown velvet. In the intimacy of the dark enclosure, they rode with averted eyes. Ruth hopefully waited for him to make some move toward her. Wouldn't he kiss her now? When it became apparent that he would not, she leaned back against the seat and, with a provocative pout which he sensed but could not see, said, "Don't be cross with me, Francis."

He sat like a statue, giving no sign of having heard her, staring into the darkness ahead.

The ride was short. Soon the coachman swung his horses into the long narrow alley that led to a large property at the back of the houses fronting Tradd Street. The silence inside the carriage was tinged with embarrassment as they rode up the driveway between the high walls to the front door of the residence.

This was the house given by Rawlins Lowndes to his daughter. The bridegroom had furnished it handsomely with the usual appointments of the period: damask draperies, English furniture, crystal chandeliers, oriental rugs, satin chairs and sofas. It was brightly lit for the coming of its new mistress; the slaves were standing in line to welcome the bride and groom.

As Francis took her hand to help her from the coach, Ruth responded to the assurance of his touch. When he ceremoniously led her to the door, she paused in anticipation, holding out her arms to be taken up and carried over the threshold. She meant to clasp her hands around his neck and hold fast until she forced his lips to respond to hers.

Francis stood stiffly beside her. Ignoring her gesture, he bowed formally and said, "I hope you will find everything to your liking, Ma'am."

"So!" she flared. "So!" Her proud eyes flashed, she held her head high, and her voice rang out clear and cool and indifferent, "I shall indeed! Goodnight to you, Sir."

She walked swiftly through the doorway and up the stairs without a backward glance, but she heard the hoofbeats as the carriage took him away. The slaves stared in big-eyed wonder and began to giggle among themselves.

Ruth entered the bridal chamber, a spacious room, luxuriously furnished, and bright with candlelight. The maids came in, bobbing respectfully, and began to undress her. She did not speak, and they did not dare break the silence, seeing the trembling lips and the angry eyes. She almost lost her self-control when they slipped over her head the nightgown of finest muslin she had embroidered with joyful anticipation.

The slaves helped her into the high bed, raised a window, and, blowing out all the candles except one, curtsied good night. They rushed out to join in the gossiping at the slave quarters.

With relief she saw them go. In the big four-poster bed, she lay and stared dry-eyed at the strange room. A fresh breeze stirred the bed hangings, and the flickering candle made grotesque shadows that advanced and retreated in menacing weirdness. The silence oppressed her, reminding her that she was alone in the house with its unknown spaces and numerous rooms.

"Alone," the silence seemed to say. The slave quarters were some distance from the house. "Alone." Never had she been by herself at night before.

"Alone," the word repeated itself in her brain like the tolling of a bell. "Alone, alone, alone." And she had lived for, and longed for, this night.

It could not be true; it must be a bad dream. He had never said that he loved her, that she well knew. She had flirted with him, teased him, tried with all of woman's wiles to get from him some sign of affection—some word or some little gesture that she could interpret as love. But there, like a barrier between them, was his quiet, gentle dignity. She had been forced to make some move!

She had loved Francis so long she couldn't say when it had first begun. As time passed, her feeling for him mounted and she knew there was nothing she would not do to become his wife. It never occurred to her that he would not be deliriously happy once they were married.

She rememberd the day of the oyster roast at his plantation on John's Island when for the first time he showed an interest in Sabina Smith. It was especially annoying since she, Ruth, planned to marry Francis, and Dick Johnston was expected to marry Sabina. There was no sense in upsetting everything because Francis suddenly found Sabina attractive.

That lovely day under a clear blue sky tables had been set before the spreading house with its wide piazzas. The small Negro boys ran busily here and there with platters of hot oysters which they cracked open for guests. She had gone with the usual hopeful expectations, and Francis had sat between Sabina and her. She had introduced Sabina as her closest friend, but that was no reason why he should have given her his whole attention. Afterwards, Francis and Sabina had walked together beside the river.

The shadows came and went as the candle flickered in "the bridal chamber."

Only yesterday he had accused her of "tricking" him into marriage. How ridiculous! She had only helped him, because he was shy and it seemed that he would never speak. If it had not been for the handkerchief, she would not be married to him now. She laughed to herself. It had really been so easy. And how cleverly she had done it, knowing that once he was committed he would rather die than break his word!

All went as she had planned. Their engagement had been announced. If only he had not discovered her maneuvering before the wedding, then the handkerchief would not have mattered.

Once more the dark shadows, the flickering candle, and the silence reminded her she was alone. Was it possible that she could be a married spinster for the rest of her days? Oh no—no—no— She would never forgive him for that. She hated him—hated him! Sitting up, she beat her hands on the bed in the violence of her emotion.

Then, when her passion was spent, she saw once more his gentle eyes and his charming smile and in an agony of despair, she longed for his love.

Love—she had been willing to pay the price for it. Had she not bought everything else she wanted?

But what if she had only gained—nothing? Oh no, not nothing. He was her husband. Hers—whether he liked it or not. Forever and forever hers. No other woman, Sabina or any other, would have him. Ruth Simmons thereupon made up her mind that she would live a long, long time. She began to laugh. It would be her joke after all. "How funny, how very funny—!"

Next morning she was calm and resolved to make the best of a bad bargain. She would create a romance about the mystery of the quarrel to fill people's minds. It would be "Poor little abandoned bride, and all over a silly quarrel. What a stupid boor Francis Simmons must have been!"

And thus it was. She went everywhere, gracious always, apparently carefree and happy, and her laughter rang out pleasantly on all occasions. To her husband she was unfailingly courteous and exasperatingly indifferent. And so began the intriguing mystery which gave her a romantic aura that lasted for generations.

Francis Simmons presided at her dinners and attended her receptions. It gave him some bitter satisfaction to appear formally as master of the house. Between Ruth and Francis Simmons was a defiant attitude; each felt the sweet victory of having bettered the other. And always, Mr. Simmons left with the last guests. He did not live at 131 Tradd Street.

Of an afternoon, when they went for a drive around the Battery—she in her fine coach and he in his new curricle—they would bow elaborately, and he could be heard to say, "How do you do, Ma'am?"

"And you, Sir?"

Each would smile with secret satisfaction.

Francis still lived at his plantation on John's Island. After five years passed in this manner, he decided he needed a city home—perhaps to prove publicly that he did not live with his wife, or perhaps because he found it troublesome—particularly in bad weather—to have his slaves bring him to town by canoe. Then, too, he led a lonely life and he must have wanted to be nearer his friends and family, of whom he was very fond.

At 14 Legare Street, he found a good property for sale and acquired it at a reasonable price. He proceeded to tear down the inadequate structure and build a house of enduring beauty. Its creation constituted all of the allotment of happiness left Francis in life. For the next few years he was completely absorbed in the building of *Brick House*. All too soon it was done, and when he had furnished it handsomely, he moved in.

But once more the loneliness he dreaded closed around him, and he sat in his elegant drawing room to brood upon his frustrated life. He pictured how different it could be if the rooms were filled with the voices of a wife he loved and of children.

Some days he thought about his early childhood. How singularly happy they had been despite the war, for he had been fortunate in the companionship of his brothers and his sister Ann. They had fished in the river and roamed in the woods nearby and played games under the spreading oaks. There had always been the shadow of the war, of course. As a boy he had heard the frightened slaves say, "De British air comin'." Presently the redcoats left the island, and then for a while his mother's troubles seemed to be lightened, until Lord Rawdon sent for his father to come to Charles Town where he was thrown into prison and eventually died.

Times had become hard for them after that. His mother had made a gallant struggle to keep the crops planted and the family fed. It was tidewater rice that had saved the place for them. In a few more years they had means enough again to provide for luxuries.

He remembered with a warm rush of feeling his pretty sister Ann, who was gone now, too. He had been her favorite brother. She had always been doing something to please him such as embroidering the handkerchief. She never suspected her loving handiwork would be his undoing.

With the handkerchief he had been caught like a fly in a web. His mother had taught him that honor demanded "that a man's word must be better than his bond. A woman's name must never pass his lips except in respect; a promise, however foolish, must be kept." Honor was more important than life, itself. He thought bitterly how this did not seem to apply to a woman. Ruth could deceive and be respected for the rest of her days.

Too late he had discovered her perfidy. Yet he had been honor-bound to keep his word. In his rage, he had gone to her and accused her, and she had looked at him in bland surprise. It was incredible to her that he could be angry with her. She had even pretended to be hurt.

This memory always filled his heart with rebellion, which would pass as he gloated over his revenge. For she was a spinster still—with no husband, no children. He would never touch her.

Season after season passed, and one summer afternoon Francis was sitting in the high-backed wing chair beside the front window in his drawing room. Outside, the trees blew wildly with a coming storm, but Francis scarcely noticed. He was expecting a more fateful event. His will had been made leaving his possessions to his nieces and nephews, his cousins, and his friends. To his wife he left nothing; he had settled fifteen hundred pounds on her at the "time of their separation." Twenty years of longing had passed. Now that Sabina was dead, it was a meaningless, empty world. There was little to live for, and he was thankful that his loneliness would soon be ended.

In the deepening darkness of the storm, he sat and stared before him, his thoughts going back, as always, to the memories he cherished. Lovely Sabina, dear Sabina! The times with her had been all too few, and he must dream over them, for they were his only consolation.

He liked to remember the day when he had first realized her beauty and charm. He had sat between Sabina and Ruth and soon had forgotten Ruth's existence. His whole world had suddenly centered on the gentle, gray-eyed girl. After feasting on oysters, they had gotten up to walk to the river's edge. He could still see the sunlight on Sabina's blond hair, turning it to gold against the cloudless blue of the sky. He could remember her shapely nose and the enchanted smile on her sweet lips.

She had said, "Your place is so beautiful. I will never forget it as I have seen it today."

Francis remembered he had wanted to say, "Forget it? Ah, my dear, I only want to give it to you so that you will know it always." He smiled at the recollection.

Then he frowned at another memory. It was the day before the wedding. Hurrying down Church Street, he passed the Smith house. The front door was open on the piazza, and Sabina was coming in from the garden. It was a warm day in November, and in her hand was the last rose of the autumn. Her eyes were sad and moist with tears.

Seeing him pause, she stopped in surprise and managed a sort of smile as she said, "I hope you will be very happy."

"Thank you," he said. "I wish the same to you. When will you be married?"

"I? Married? You are joking, Sir."

"What do you mean?"

"I have no intention of marrying." And as he stared at her speechlessly, she said, "You are teasing, of course."

"No. I was told that you had given your promise to Dick Johnston and that your engagement would be announced soon."

"Never! I would not dream of marrying him. Who could have told you such a thing?"

"Who?" Francis echoed her question. "Who, indeed?" Then he cried, "My God, what a fool I've been!"

"How could you have believed it?"

"From your closest friend it was quite convincing."

She stared at him helplessly, and in that moment much became clear to her.

He moved close to her, and in a voice hoarse with emotion said, "You must know that I love you. I will never love anyone but you. It is true. I would never have consented to marry her had I not been convinced that you were lost to me." He choked and could not speak. Then he cried out, "She even pictured you ridiculing my love. She quoted unkind things that you had said about me."

"No, Francis, it is not true." Her voice was trembling as she whispered, "I have always loved you."

With a quick step, he closed the door to the street and turning, took her in his arms.

She clung to him, sobbing, as he stroked her soft hair and murmured, "What a fool I have been, what a fool!"

When she withdrew from his embrace to wipe away the tears from her cheeks, she saw the tragic look on his face.

"God help me, I am honor-bound to marry the daughter of Rawlins Lowndes," he said.

She nodded and could not speak.

"It was the handkerchief," he cried in despair. "The one Ann embroidered for me. So small a thing. I—I, Dear God, I showed it to Ruth, and I was so proud of it, I said, 'Wouldn't you like to have such beautiful initials?' " He stared hopelessly at Sabina. He still could not understand why fate had singled him out for its bitter game.

"Next day Rawlins Lowndes sent for me. He said he understood that I had proposed to his daughter. I could not bring myself to insult the old gentleman, and since you were lost to me, I did not really care," his voice trailed off. Then the anger returned like a flash and he cried, "She will never be my wife, never!"

He sealed his vow by pressing to his heart Sabina's hand, thereby crushing the rose she held.

"Neither will I ever marry," said Sabina.

Francis took her in his arms and kissed her upon the lips.

Afterwards, she turned from him and ran swiftly into the house, leaving at his feet the scattered rose petals.

At the Legare Street house, the rain beat against the panes, streaking strange patterns on the glass. Inside, the drawing room had a special insulation against the noise of the wild elements and the hurt of painful memories; for its only occupant sat slumped in his chair, dead.

On Tradd Street, there is no house now at Number 131; handsome brick columns mark the entrance to a long narrow alley. Here, in the small hours of the night, when all of Charleston is quiet with sleep, one is startled to hear the pounding of horses' hoofs and the rumbling of wheels as though a coach is passing in the alley.

Old-timers say, "It is only Ruth Simmons driving to her empty marriage bed."

Medway's Ghosts

M edway, a place of enchantment two miles above Goose Creek, is approached by a driveway bordered with massive live oaks filmy with moss. Hide-and-seek glimpses of the house in the distance fail to prepare one for the effect at closer view. The ancient dwelling, with an expanse of lawn spreading to the river under more oaks, has muted brownish-pink shutters and brick walls of the same melancholy color.

The oldest house of record in the state, it was constructed of brick made and dried on the place in 1686, sixteen years after the Charles Town colony was founded. A mellow grandeur clings to the walls Jan Van Arrsens, Seigneur de Weirnhoudt, built for his beautiful wife, Sabina de Vignon. The stairstep gables remind one of the tradition in Brittany, just across the channel from Van Arrsens' Holland, that gables so fashioned induced evil spirits to walk down and leave the house in peace.

MEDWAY

*"The stairstep gables . . . induced evil spirits to walk down
and leave the house in peace."*

Jan did not live long to enjoy his wife and home. His widow married Landgrave Thomas Smith, who served as governor of the Carolinas. They had no children, but when Landgrave Smith died at the age of forty-six and was buried at Medway, two sons by a former marriage survived.

While Smith's grave is marked by a heavy slab, there is no trace of the grave of Van Arrsens.

The Dutchman, undaunted, returns to assert his possession, however. Anyone who is bold enough to sleep in the bedroom upstairs on the south side, a part of the original structure, may wake in the night to see him seated before the fireplace smoking his pipe. He seems to be relishing both his pipe and his home, caring not a hoot for Landgrave Smith and his many descendants who peopled the state.

Perhaps he is making up for the householding deprived him by his early death. Or he may come back to *Medway* with contentment because later owners have been inspired with his own architectural taste. Additions to *Medway* from time to time have all been in keeping with the original home built by the Dutchman who savors his pipe yet in the south bedroom.

Downstairs, there is another ghostly visitor—a beautiful girl whose heart was broken as she stood by the north window waiting for her young husband's return.

Many hunts have been held at *Medway*, and once a gay gathering of deer hunters and their wives included a newly wed couple very much in love.

The girl was reluctant to let her young husband go. She begged that he stay with her, but he had no idea of missing the excitement of the hunt. Laughing at her fears, he kissed her fondly and went off into the woods with the other hunters.

His bride watched him go with a foreboding of disaster. Through the long hours of waiting she was distracted, her restless, dark eyes betraying her anxiety. She took no part in the laughter and gaiety around her but continually went to the north window to look out toward the woods. The others joked, and coaxed, but she only smiled gently and went back to look once more through the small panes until at last, dusk began to gray the sky and trees.

Eventually the hunters returned, not with laughter and banter as when they had gone out, but with downcast eyes and reluctant tread. Two of the party were carrying an improvised stretcher.

The girl's eyes sought frantically for the face she loved. Only when the stretcher was placed at her feet did she see whose lifeless form lay there.

They took her home where she died shortly afterward. All the years since, she has haunted the spot where she died in fact— at the sight of a face on a stretcher at *Medway*. Night after night she comes back to the place of her anguish to wait for her husband.

Some say the hunter's young bride comes and stands there by the north window to gaze through the small panes. Others say there is only the rustling of her gown as she waits, like a deer moving a branch in the forest.

The Wager
of "Mad Archie" Campbell

C aptain Campbell walked briskly in the cool night. He even swaggered a bit, for Captain Campbell, an officer in the king's army, was on his way to a ball where he would see his lovely Paulina.

The captain stroked his chin with his hand and his lips twitched as he imagined the lady capitulating at last. It was high time that she ceased her banter and listened to his protestations. But women were like that—they must keep a man waiting and guessing, pretending not to be eager.

What a feminine piece she was! Her fragility delighted him, and her coyness intrigued him. A little minx she was, to pretend not to understand his wooing. Egad, he liked them innocent. He wanted a wife who would look up to him in all things. His Paulina was not the demanding kind. She was sweet and unspoiled.

St. Michael's chimed and he hastened his steps on down Meeting Street and turned the corner of Ladson. Here he paused in the narrow street to look up at the handsome residence at Number 2.

The windows were ablaze with light, and the close street echoed with the sounds of merriment. Fiddles scraped tunefully above the accompaniment of the piano, making the tempo for the measured pointing and bowing of the minuet. Mingled with the music were the hum of many voices and occasional peals of laughter.

"Mad Archie" sprang up the steps and, giving his cockaded tricorn to the butler, went into the drawing room to bow low over the hand of his hostess, Mrs. Tidyman.

Captain Campbell found many friends to greet in this distinguished gathering of Britishers and Tories, for the year was 1780 when the Royalists were occupying Charles Town. The ladies were all Tories; although every means was tried to induce the Whig ladies to attend, not one ever appeared at a Tory ball.

The captain, conscious of his good looks in his white breeches and gold-braided red coat, cast a searching eye over the throng. The lady he sought was not there; he therefore passed through the hall and up the broad carpeted stairs to the ballroom above.

Almost at once he found her. Her white panniered gown swayed gracefully as she bowed and turned in the steps of the dance. The toss of her curls would have caught the eye of any man, for Paulina Phelps was beautiful, and, as the richness of her dress and the jewels at her throat proclaimed, a lady of wealth as well.

Archie frowned as he saw the coquettish glances she gave her tall blond partner. When the dance was over and Archie bowed to claim the pleasure of the next, she declared sweetly that it was already taken. His rival smiled with smug satisfaction.

Archie stood and watched in mounting rage. Of friends who joined him, he demanded, "Who is this young puppy?"

"The new lieutenant from Philadelphia. Challenge him, Archie, the young upstart. This is effrontery."

"Never mind," said Captain Campbell. "I intend to marry the lady."

A burst of laughter drowned out his words and he had to raise his voice, "I shall challenge him, but first I shall be married."

"Married? In faith, it looks as if the wedding will not be yours."

"Gentlemen, you intimate this popinjay could win her from me?"

Their eyes turned to see Paulina smile bewitchingly at the badly smitten lieutenant.

"I'll wager—" began one of Archie's friends, but Archie cried, "Nay, gentlemen. It is I who will wager—my Arab filly to your fifty pounds—that within three days I will be married to the lady." And at their scoffing rejoinders, he added, "And with her consent."

"Taken, taken!" they cried and shook hands on it.

It was a time of much wagering. A man would bet his possessions on the slightest whim with reckless disregard of consequences. Even so, Archie's friends thought it a pity thus to forfeit the Arabian horse of which he was so justly proud. It seemed misfortune enough to lose the lady.

Next day, in the sunshine of early afternoon, Captain Campbell drove up to the door of 43 East Battery. He had come to invite "Miss Polly" to go for a drive in his fashionable gig behind his spirited steed. Miss Phelps sent back word that she would be pleased to go. She was unable to resist the chance to show herself in a gig, the mere ownership of which was considered proof of respectability.

She donned her blue cloak and her prettiest bonnet with the plumes, and graciously allowed Captain Campbell to assist her into the high seat. It seemed most exciting.

They drove rapidly. Soon the town was left behind and they were in the country. Now Archie urged the filly to greater speed. She reared and plunged, and raced madly, over rough roads, banks, ditches, mud holes—faster and faster.

Paulina protested, "Oh, Sir! Could we go a little slower?"

"Ah, Miss Polly. It is lovely to see your eyes so large and to feel your hand upon my arm. You are so pretty, and your lips are so red and my steed does so love to run. He will not listen to reason. Reason, Miss Polly? Who cares for reason? It is glorious to ride with you, like flying, Miss Polly, my sweet. Let us fly together to the skies!"

"But, Captain Campbell, I—"

"No, 'buts', my lovely. On and on we go—to the road that has no turning."

And virtually flying they went until at last they reached the church at Goose Creek. Archie drew up at the door of the rectory and Mr. Ellington came out. Paulina, half-fainting, was helped from the gig.

When she had recovered, with the kind ministrations of the parson, Archie announced to that gentleman that they had come to be married.

The good man, bewildered, protested, "Not without the consent of the lady."

Whereupon Mad Archie, living up to his name, drew his pistol, shouting, "Unless you comply, you shall be instantly shot, and the lady's virtue could only suffer in consequence. I say, Sir. Make haste!" And pointing another pistol at Paulina, he said with a charming smile, "The lady does consent. Do you not, my dear?"

"Yes—! Oh, yes!" she stammered, trembling, and hurriedly repeated the marriage vows as Mr. Ellington lined them out.

When it was done and they were man and wife, Archie became the solicitous husband and drove her back to town at a moderate pace.

The happy bride told her family of her marriage, declaring, "Until we arrived at Goose Creek, I had never thought seriously of marrying Captain Campbell. Indeed, I supposed his wild talk to be only a soldier's way of making love."

Mad Archie won his wager, fifty pounds, and his beautiful bride. But his happiness was short-lived, for within the year he was captured in a skirmish at Videau's Bridge; later, while riding behind his captor, he tried to escape and was shot dead.

Paulina and Archie spent their short life together at *Exeter* Plantation where she died soon afterwards.

There, of a night, when an eerie stillness creeps over the old place, a stealthy rustling can be heard as of someone moving. Some say it is dried leaves stirred by the wind, and some, that Paulina passes—poor Paulina seeking the tiny baby she left behind her.

XVI

In the bright cheerful room
he had come to say good-bye

The Ghost in the Library

On a day in January, 1805, Maria Heyward retired to the pleasant library of the house at 31 Legare Street so the servants could finish clearing away the morning meal. During this customarily enjoyable interlude before beginning the daily routine of housekeeping, Maria, in a leisurely way, worked bright threads into a design of flowers on a piece of linen. The sunlight streamed in from the high windows on the south, brightening her white neckerchief and the frilled cap on her soft curls.

Sitting in her favorite spot here in the bay she could see the trees against the sky and, from the east windows, the dark magnolias in the garden of Madame Talvande's school across the street.

Maria and her brothers, James and William, had grown up at *Old House* plantation, but fourteen years before, when their father had died, their mother had purchased a double lot on Legare Street. The house she had built defied conventional

Charleston architecture by having the piazzas located on the east, rather than on the south where the sea breezes blew. The break with tradition had made the library a particularly bright and cheerful room in winter.

Maria had just taken up a blood-red skein of embroidery thread and was preparing to thread her needle, when her younger brother came into the room. She put down her work and smiled at the sight of James.

He was slight, and picturesque-looking in his buff-colored breeches and dark green coat. And that ridiculous hat with the bird's feather stuck in the band, how jauntily it sat on the side of his head, exposing one dark lock on his forehead.

"James is such an attractive boy," she thought. "Some men are grown up and married at eighteen, but James is still Mama's baby. Now that William is gone, she will try to keep him as long as she can."

James hummed softly as he came over to kiss his sister on the cheek. "Where are you bound for this morning?" she asked casually.

"Plantation on the Euhaws," he answered. "I'll be late. Don't expect me for dinner." And, bowing with a wave of his hat, he said, "Prepare, Ma'am, to eat venison."

"James, do be careful."

"Nonsense," he scoffed. "I am no baby."

"But you look so young," she thought as she smiled at him affectionately.

He went outside, mounted his horse, and rode off to join his friends.

The morning passed slowly for Maria, though there was much for her to do. The responsibility of running the house had been hers ever since William had eloped with the Cruger girl and her mother had taken to her bed.

When all was attended to and she was free at last to come back to the wood-paneled library, it was midday, but there was still time to write letters before dinner.

She entered the room and started for the desk when, to her surprise, she saw James seated there. He wore the green coat and the hunting hat and sat with his head on his hand as though he were tired.

"Why, James!" she cried. "What are you doing back here so soon?"

Before her eyes he vanished.

She was gripped by some force that seemed to stay her steps as she stared in disbelief at the empty chair. There was no one there, and yet she had been so certain James was present that she had spoken to him.

"How strange! How very strange!" She shivered.

With wildly beating heart, she turned and ran from the room. Her trembling hands sought little tasks to occupy them, her teeming brain tried unsuccessfully to avoid the haunting memory of the vision.

They found the horse first. There was blood on the saddle. After a long search they found the body. Apparently, the dogs had become excited and bayed at a hog, and James, exasperated, had struck at them with the butt of his gun. The weapon discharged, and a bullet lodged in his neck, killing him instantly.

Some hours later, they brought the body home. The spirited boy who had gone out so full of joyous expectations had been felled by one small gesture. James was gone forever.

"What time did it happen?" Maria finally asked.

"It must have been just at midday," she was told.

She knew then, as she already had sensed, that her brother's spirit, in departing, had sought her there in the library where they had said good-bye.

James's spirit lingers still in the room where Maria last saw him. Once, when an elderly gentleman who became the owner entered the library, he was startled to find a man, roughly attired in a green hunting coat, sitting at the desk. Since the intruder was leaning over and apparently did not see him, the owner stole away to obtain a weapon with which to defend himself.

Having secured a poker from the next room, he returned immediately, prepared to oust the stranger. The man was gone, although he could not have left by the hall without being seen.

In recent years, on an occasion when a child was ill in the house, the family waited impatiently for the arrival of the doctor. The butler, passing the door to the library, saw a man seated at the desk and hurried to tell the parents that the doctor had come. The father rushed to the room to urge the physician to go to the sick child's bedroom at once, but no one was there.

The butler, stupefied, protested, "He bin dar. Yassir, he sho' bin dar. I scen him wid me own eye, asettin' dar wid he green coat and he hat push back on he head. He res' he head on he han' lak he tired."

The Sword Gates Romance

A t 39 Legare Street stands a high brick wall. Its tall columns support handsome iron gates fashioned in a somewhat forbidding design of crossed swords and spears.

The wall and the Sword Gate have not always so shielded the garden and dwelling there. For many years after the house was built in 1776, only a hedge and a wooden gate stood between the flower beds and the street. Inside was a girls' school conducted by Madame Talvande where "young women were taught to be ladies." They learned, besides their lessons, "absolute submission to the will of the teacher, which would astonish the young people of the present day," according to Mrs. St. Julien Ravenel writing in 1906.[1]

To the school in 1828 came 15-year-old Maria Whaley, whose flashing eyes and smile had made a Mr. George Morris dissatisfied with his heretofore confirmed state of bachelorhood.

---

[1] Ravenel, *Charleston, the Place and the People* (New York: Macmillan Company, 1912).

Colonel Joseph Whaley had forbidden his daughter's suitor to enter the premises of *Pine Baron Plantation* on Edisto Island and requested that no door be opened to him on the island. But Mr. Morris, undismayed, had set up a tent and camped near the plantation, continuing his courtship of Maria when she went riding. The exasperated parent at length decided to send his daughter to the Talvande school to put an end to the affair. There the weeks and months dragged by for Maria.

On the eighth day of March that year a coast storm had brought rain, and when night fell, Charleston's muddy streets were dark and cold. A fitful wind teased the hat and cloak from anyone foolish enough to be about. An occasional light could be seen through the trees, or from a window on the street; but it was out of the ordinary when, at this hour, a light appeared in St. Michael's church.

The uncertain candlelight inside the church revealed a group of people waiting: Mr. Dalcho, the minister, in his robes; and a few ladies and gentlemen. The latter, in cloaks held close about them to ward off the chill, watched with affectionate amusement as one of their number, a relative, paced up and down.

It was not the cold that kept George Morris moving, but nervousness and fear that some unforeseen happening might prevent his bride from coming. His good friend, Mrs. Blank, had promised to bring her, but it was possible that Maria had not been able to get away from the school.

A clatter of hoofs broke the silence; then a carriage came to a sudden stop out front. All turned to look as Mrs. Blank entered, followed by two young girls. In a diary left by a Morris relative, the lady is unnamed, but tradition maintains that the bridesmaid was Miss Sarah Seabrook.

The happy Mr. Morris rushed to meet his bride-to-be.

After the brief ceremony, the witnesses, like the conspirators they were, smiled and nodded in satisfaction and departed in haste. George and his bride, having received Mr. Dalcho's blessing, entered the coach with Mrs. Blank, for that lady, while she had agreed to bring the bride and be a party to the wedding, would have none of a midnight elopement. Her stipulation was that the girl must return to the school and leave it properly in the daytime.

The bride and groom held hands as they rode in emotion-packed silence the three blocks to the school. The coach drew up to the wooden gates and stopped. Mrs. Blank pressed Maria's hand affectionately; Sarah kissed her, and George helped her to alight.

For a moment they stood in the shadow of the hedge where he embraced her tenderly and whispered, "Tomorrow, my love," and, parting the dripping branches, held them so that she might slip through.

There was no sound except the drip and splash of rain from the magnolia trees as Maria stood, knowing only the singing of her heart, when, suddenly, there was a movement in the shrubbery beside her.

Frightened, Maria ran blindly for the front door. She did not see the puddle, nor care, but her foot slipped, and as she fell, she felt wet earth on her hands and mud splashing in her face.

Up again, she stumbled on, rushed up the steps and tried the front door. It was unlocked, and Maria pushed it open and stepped quickly inside.

She almost fell into the arms of Miss Hanburn who had charge of the girls at night, and stared at Maria's condition in speechless surprise. The beautiful white dress was a hopeless rag. Black mud clung to it from the softly pleated bodice down the long skirt to her drenched, satin-clad toes. Muddy water dripped in puddles on the floor as she faced the questioning eyes of the teacher.

Then, shivering with fright and cold, she began to sob, "Oh, Miss Hanburn, I—I fell. I'm so wet, so cold—" Her teeth were chattering.

The woman was immediately concerned. "My dear child, what on earth? Come quickly. Let me help you. You'll be catching your death of cold."

The kind-hearted spinster ran to get warm milk and medicine and a hot brick to put at Maria's feet. There was no time for questions, and the little bride was tucked away in bed and told to keep warm and to go to sleep.

And so she did, with a happy smile in the knowledge that she was married and no one could change that wonderful fact. No one—no matter how angry he might be!

In the morning, a coach drove up to the wooden gates of the school and George Morris stepped out. He pulled the bell boldly and seemed to enjoy its clanging. When a maid opened the door, he asked for Mrs. Morris.

But the maid said, "Ain't nebber hear tell ob de lady." Mr. Morris insisted that she was within. He finally demanded to be taken to Madame Talvande.

Upon being admitted and received by that personage, he announced once more that he had come for Mrs. Morris. He said it as though he liked the sound of it.

"Sir, there is no one here by that name," said the headmistress.

But, upon his very positive insistence, Miss Hanburn and the girls were all assembled. Madame Talvande, with some irony and an amused smile, addressed the girls: "This gentleman has come for his wife, and he is certain that she is here," she said. "Is anyone of you, by any *possible* chance, Mrs. Morris?"

Maria stepped demurely forward and dropped a curtsy.

Madame cried, "What is the meaning of this? Your father did not advise me that you were married."

"He does not know it," said Maria. "We were married last evening in St. Michael's Church." And, looking at Mr. Morris, she blushed and dropped her eyes before his gaze.

Miss Hanburn became hysterical and had to be taken from the room.

Maria drove off in the coach with her husband and tactfully avoided her irate parent until his anger cooled. Like the princess in the fairy tale, she lived happily ever after. Her father eventually forgave her and generously provided her with money, for he "could not bear to have her dependent on anyone."

Madame Talvande, to save the reputation of the school, then built the high wall that now hides the garden. It had wooden gates until 1838, when the city fathers placed an order for grille work for the newly built guardhouse. The gates, a part of this order, were rejected as being too costly and were secured by Madame for the entrance to the school.

They now guard the delightful garden of a private residence, as the property was sold in 1849; but for eleven years they successfully served their purpose, for there were no more elopements from Madame Talvande's school.

At night a ghost walks the halls. She comes into the south bedroom upstairs, and there she vanishes. Is this Madame Talvande herself, fearful that another girl will get beyond the walls? Or is it poor Miss Hanburn who cannot rest after being duped by young Maria Whaley?

Alone, at last, they heard
Pinky's playful rat-a-taps

XVIII

Pinky

L avinia lived alone on the third floor of an old Charleston
house. She liked living up there because there were too
many steps for Aunt Carrie and Aunt Vinnie to climb, and
she was out of the way of their eternal questioning. "Why do
old maids," she wondered, "have so much curiosity about
everything?"

When her mother and father had died, Lavinia had found
a home with her father's sisters, for which she was grateful.
Nevertheless, she was sometimes annoyed—and sometimes
merely amused—by their funny questions.

Lavinia filled her rather lonely life with studying and reading and taking occasional walks along the Battery with her
friends.

One afternoon she came home at dusk and after a light
supper with her aunts, ran happily up the long flights of steps,
eager to get back to her book. Reaching the top landing, she

was startled to hear the pitapat of soft footsteps walking beside her.

Lavinia stopped and listened.

The steps ran around her and led the way to her door.

She was frightened and started to go back down to tell Aunt Carrie and Aunt Vinnie.

The steps patted again and seemed to urge her to come on.

"It is silly to be afraid," she thought. "Besides, my aunties would never believe me. They would think I was fooling and say 'Go on to bed, Child.' "

So she followed the steps and began to talk to them.

"Who are you?" she asked.

"Pat-pat-pat."

"What do you want?"

The taps ran around her.

She shut the door behind her and came into the room. Holding out her hand and smiling, she said, "Can I do anything for you?"

No sound.

"Tell me who you are," she pleaded, "so we can be friends."

The taps did a lively jig.

Lavinia sat down and laughed merrily. "What fun to have you here," she said.

Then the taps showed great delight. "Rat-a-tap, rat-a-tap." They went all the way up the wall, across the ceiling and down, to stop beside her.

After awhile the tapping died away, and Lavinia went to sleep with a happy smile. She would not be lonely any more. She named her ghost "Pinky".

Night after night Pinky came. Pinky tapped and Lavinia laughed. Her aunts questioned her about the noise and she told them that she was practicing dance steps. They were amused at the dear child's enthusiasm.

Then Lavinia fell in love. Of course, she told Pinky about it, and that was the night Pinky made a terrible fuss. "Bang—bang—bang," he stamped, up and down.

Lavinia was amazed. "Why, Pinky," she said. "You should *want* me to fall in love. Every girl hopes to fall in love. It is the happiest way to be. You wouldn't want me to grow into an old maid like Aunt Carrie or Aunt Vinnie, would you? You wouldn't even like me if I were like that!"

But Pinky continued to stamp until she put out the light and went to bed. Then all was quiet.

Whenever Lavinia hummed a love song, there was the same scene. She was careful not to mention Kenneth's name in talks with Pinky. And so the months went by until one night she told Pinky that she was going to marry Kenneth in the fall.

Pinky was really mad. He banged in one spot, stamped to another, and banged again. This went on for some time. The noise was so loud that Lavinia could not be heard. She beat her fists together. She, too, was angry. When, finally, she got a chance to speak, she told Pinky his wild antics had to stop. She would not be a friend to him any more if he behaved in that manner. She did not like him and she did not want him to come, ever again, she said.

Pinky's raps stopped. The next night Lavinia relented and tried to start up a conversation, without result. For weeks Lavinia called and coaxed. There was no answer. Pinky was gone.

Lavinia was sorry. She missed him. "Pinky," she told him night after night, "I am sorry. Don't be mad with me. Please, Pinky, come back."

Not a tap, not a sound answered her. She had lost her ghost.

The days passed quickly, for the wedding was approaching. Lavinia, busy, happy, and very much in love, forgot about Pinky. She even forgot to tell Kenneth about her funny, invisible visitor.

And so they were married. It was a simple wedding in the front parlor with a few friends and Aunt Carrie and Aunt Vinnie who were in a great state over it. In those days the honeymoon was spent at home, so the dear old ladies had spruced up the room on the third floor for the bridal couple.

When the guests were all gone, the bride and groom retired up the steep stairway with much handwaving and throwing of kisses.

At last they were alone. Lavinia sat in the big bed in her linen gown with long sleeves and frills at neck and wrists.

Kenneth, in his nightshirt, turned down the wick of the oil lamp. The room was dim and full of shadows. Immediately there was a terrific "rat-a-tap! rat-a-tap! bang! bang!" from every side.

"What the—" he said, and quickly turned up the lamp.

The room was in disorder with clothes scattered over the floor and a chair overturned. Lavinia, sitting up in bed, said, "It's just Pinky."

Kenneth sprang to his feet, saying, "I'll put him out." He called, "Here Pinky, here!"

There was a noise behind a chair and Kenneth ran to look. He snapped his fingers, "Here Pinky, that's a nice boy."

No sooner had he reached the chair than there was a "tap-tap-tap" from the wardrobe. Poking his head inside, he coaxed, "Now Pinky, come boy." But the noise was now under the bed. "Pinky, here Pinky," he called (he was down on his knees). The "rat-a-tap" could be heard from the other side of the room.

Lavinia rocked from side to side with laughter, and could not speak. At last she found her voice, "Ken," she squealed and choked. She tried once more, "Ken, Pinky is a ghost."

"A what—?"

"Pinky is my ghost."

"Don't joke with me. Let's get him out of here."

Kenneth's nightshirt was given a sudden jerk and he swore under his breath.

Lavinia got up and took her husband by the arm, "Come to bed, Ken. Don't pay any attention to Pinky. He is behaving very badly. I shall never, never like him any more. Go away, Pinky. Go away, I say."

Kenneth was being reluctantly led back to bed as Lavinia said, "See—he has gone. Blow out the light now."

All was quiet.

Kenneth blew out the lamp and reached for his bride.

This time the bed clothes were pulled off and the pillow jerked from under his head.

This time he was really angry. "This has got to stop!" he said.

"Don't mind him, Ken. Don't pay any attention. Now, go away, Pinky. Go away, I say!"

Another series of taps began, "Rat-a-tap! rat-a-tap! bang!"

"Please, Pinky. Be a good ghost. Please—"

The bridegroom remarked, "This is the damnedest wedding night a man ever spent."

"Yes, dear," said Lavinia. "Pinky's come back to stay. There is nothing we can do about it."

And so they began a life together, the three of them.